I0474161

Coaching, Training & Developing The Retail Manager

Richard Bell

Copyright © 2012 Richard Bell

All rights reserved.

ISBN-10:1478241780
ISBN-13:978-1478241782

DEDICATION

This book is dedicated to my wife, Jennifer. Thanks for putting up with an unforgiving schedule and the demands of retail over the past fifteen years.

CONTENTS

ACKNOWLEDGMENTS

A special thanks to Dave Bialota and Wayne Pracel for their leadership and guidance in the early years and Ken Haines for the latter years.

Chapter One
This Is What I'm Good At

Have you ever asked yourself why you are in retail? I am sure this thought has crossed your mind on more than one occasion. It usually crashes into your mind and emotions when working long days, working through a holiday or when a customer berates you on the phone or worse yet, in your store. There were many times over the past 20 years I have asked myself the same question.

I recall having this very conversation with a friend and store manager, Dave. After learning of my current regional management position being phased out, I found myself wondering if I belonged in retail and questioning my managerial skills. I stood in front of Dave and wondered how I would assimilate into another field or industry.

I asked Dave if he ever thought of a different job other than managing people. After a few moments of reflection, he talked about a deep level of satisfaction and energy derived from developing people and creating a positive working environment for employees.

The culmination of his thoughts can be paraphrased into everybody is good at something. Dave's "something" can be summarized in his parting words of the conversation "I like what I do; this is what I am good at." He was referring to leading people, improving processes, enhancing morale and increasing sales and profits.

The discussion illustrates a rewarding side of this tough business. You need to derive energy from the frustration and exhilaration of managing people. The recognition of frustration to exhilaration is the foundation of this book. If you accepted the challenge of managing people, it has to be what you are good at. Your skills cannot end with being a good number cruncher or delegator; you HAVE to connect with people.

Managing people in a retail environment today differs greatly than just ten years ago. The workload is greater, the hours longer, the resources including human and material less, customer demand is higher, competition greater, the talent pool dwindling and the accountability for middle management is endless.

The need to connect with people is a large, often left out, piece to the puzzle. It is not enough to simply have a position that exists for an employee. That mentality went out twenty years ago. People have to know where their position fits into the big picture and have the tools, guidance, discipline and support to get there.

A great gauge to test your current capability to connect with people is turnover of key performers. The higher the number, the less effective you are. In case you have not guessed it yet, I believe people before processes will get you where you want to be. This requires an investment of time, skill development, reflection, caring and understanding your organization's vision to reveal the full potential of your team as a collective whole.

Full Circle

The attempt to understand the retail manager's workload requires a quick look back at the last ten years. This book is not meant to be a lesson in retail philosophies or history. It is an honest look into the pressures of store management teams today.

Ten years ago, store managers in big box stores were given the flexibility and autonomy to make local market decisions. Store managers were heroes, recognized for creativity and thinking outside of the box to increase sales and heighten team morale. The tightened economy and emergence of competition ushered in a new era of control and command.

The focus on streamlining processes and top down management removed the local market capabilities of managers. The new era consisted of no room for failure, which stripped away the creative, and leadership abilities within the store. The power rose to the top of the organization. This allowed decision makers to opt for a cookie cutter approach to lead teams in unison whether they were in New York or Texas.

The top down approach began a stressed time period for managers. The pressure increased as timelines were condensed. The markets were moving at a furious pace to fight for the consumer dollar, this meant finding the sweet spot for customer spend. Along with deadlines came the inevitable fact of payroll reductions. Do more with less was the new motto. This was another brick on the shoulders of layers of management.

Suddenly, store conditions and customer service took center stage. This perfect storm was designed to make the good great, if it did not crack them first, and when it did crack them, the manager was not cut out for the new environment.

There was very little consideration given to the coaching, training and development of a manager to adapt to the new environment, there just wasn't time. You were told to get on board and be committed to customer service or out you go. This was considered a good thing; it allowed store managers to get rid of dead weight as headcount was reduced. The manager could simply say, "He didn't fit into our new mold." Let's face it, the managers chosen to leave, should have been gone long ago. Why weren't they? Simply, it was easier to keep them. In essence, the managerial struggle was part handed down and part self induced.

The economy continued its slow recovery in 2011 and retailers were looking to reshuffle the deck. Change management and organizational development were the buzzwords and various restructurings began.

This has brought us full circle back to concepts of ten years ago. Store managers were told they would be given local market control and the ability to tell the top brass what they think, just as they had in the past. This is a commitment, which will require a difficult and long transition for organizations.

The transition is usually based on new concepts of leadership, customer relationships, sales driven environments and valuing people. The changes, at times, lack the commitment of valuing people. This lack of people focus can create a variety of problems at the store level, discussed in later chapters.

The similarities in this circle, ten years ago store managers were considered leaders and visionaries out of rank, people had to respect their position. There were not a lot of other employment options since it was a narrower field. This led to little regard for developing or connecting with people.

Today, managers execute directives more than lead, which delays the potential transition from a manager to leader. They have become caught up in trying to get as much physically done in a day with less resources which leaves very little time to directly invest in developing or connecting with people.

The new environment has created a love and hate relationship when it comes to retail competition. When you are working for a retailer, you hate the competition for taking your sales share. The other side of that is when you are working, or no longer working, for a retailer. There are many options for employees to work somewhere else. Your employees are very aware of the opportunities. Keep disregarding the need to connect with people, your turnover numbers will continue to rise.

Not All Bad

It would be easy to blame organizational levels of control for every problem but that is not necessarily the case. Store managers may be limited with control in some areas but they have influence over many store factors. The store manager sets the tone for morale, processes, commitment and customer service levels. The local level management is exposed to many variables and the way they handle them makes a difference.

In many ways, I do not blame the organization for exercising control. It is not all bad. It takes the guesswork out of merchandising and policies and may streamline processes. There are many things you, in the store, cannot control. This book is about what you can control. Retail is not an easy gig but can be very rewarding when you get the right wheels in motion.

Connecting With People

I have said it a few times already you must connect with people. What does it mean? Connecting is showing a true and genuine interest in the lives of your managers and employees.

You cannot manage solely by the numbers. There is a need to understand the current state of business and the past to uncover opportunities in the future. Analytics have their place in the retail environment but it is difficult for people to feel appreciated or a sense of belonging when this is their basis for interaction.

Managing by the numbers creates a minimalistic workforce view. Essentially, the team will only execute the basics to meet the demand for a better performance. This allows them to avoid disciplinary measures and as their resentment grows, they will eventually avoid you.

This also creates an environment of "never enough." Employees feel their work is unappreciated, their contributions minimized and the quest to satisfy numbers will never be met. The end result is typically high turnover and failed management.

Connecting with people is not a time consuming practice. Most managers are on the sales floor a good portion of their day. The way to connect with people is by simple, short conversations. It can be discussing the status of a sales contest, great examples of their customer service, maybe a great idea they have for business, etc. It does not always have to be business based. The conversations could be around cars, animals, vacations, sports, etc. General, light conversations that make your team feel more important than task drivers.

This practice must be handled with sensitivity and professionalism. This is not a free pass to engage in conversations about risky subject matter. Be smart and engage your teams wisely. If you cross the line, it may lead to undesirable results for you such as termination.

Avoid conversations about sex, religion, ethnic and racial connotations. Do not get invasive and do not tell or listen to jokes, my advice is to avoid jokes all together. Very few exclude offensive material and if you engage in this behavior than you are condoning it. There is more about this topic in the Guard Your Words and Actions segment.

So why connect with people? Simply, if you care about the people that work for you, they will be more apt to work harder to drive for results, the work environment means more to them. The goal is working towards the organization's vision. Your people will contribute more and go beyond the minimum to achieve it. They are a part of the team, they matter, their opinion counts. You and your staff have included them in achieving results.

You will ultimately fail to achieve goals if you do not create a positive environment. You need your employees as much as they need you, just for different reasons. You need to manage right down the middle.

There are some words of caution when it comes to connecting with people. We discussed using common sense when engaging in conversations. An old supervisor of mine used to tell me common sense is different for everyone.

Here are some clarifications for connecting with people.

✓<u>Do</u> talk about business and general interest. Keep in mind employees like to talk about what is important to them.

✓<u>Do</u> make the conversations short and simple.

✓<u>Do</u> this with consistency; make it habit for you and your management staff.

✓<u>Do Not</u> discuss anything intensely personal. If the conversation requires a more in depth discussion, consider having it with your HR manager present and off the sales floor.

✓<u>Do Not</u> discuss anything of a sexual or religious nature.

✓<u>Do Not</u> engage in racially or ethnically motivated discussions.

✓<u>Do Not</u> tell or listen to jokes.

✓<u>Do Not</u> coach or discipline during these conversations. If you do this, an employee will fear having a discussion with you.

This should not be misinterpreted as going overboard and being too soft. The intent is not to be popular or liked by everyone. This leads to another set of problems. It is meant to offset accountability and development and create a balanced workplace. This balance will help to retain employees and encourage a higher level of productivity.

Managing Down the Middle

The art of connecting with people is a necessity to succeed in managing a retail team. I call it an art because not everyone possess the ability to do this well. There has to be more to the environment than pure accountability. Accountability is important and is included in many places throughout this book but it cannot be a singular approach.

This art is challenged in the face of variables and extremes. On one hand you have a manager that rules with an iron fist and on the other is a manager that is preoccupied with being liked or too soft, like a marshmallow. Both of these situations pose a problem with a design for failure.

The solution to these two dilemmas is managing down

the middle. Not easy, especially for new managers, these challenges are common traps. Managing down the middle is finding the balance of accountability and relating to people. Both must exist in proportion as dictated by the store environment. A struggling or broken store may require more of one side than the other. A well-balanced store may require a shift as the environment changes.

Shifts often occur between the two depending on the current state of the environment. The environment could be stabile right now as you are working on accountability but two key staff members could leave and shift the environment.

The two extremes are created from an imbalance in accountability and relationships with people. You cannot be on the sidelines and be effective. You need to have a balance to achieve the organizations vision, right down the middle.

The Marshmallow

This represents the soft side of managing people. The manager is preoccupied with being liked and derives a level of satisfaction from being popular with people. They feel this outward concern and willingness to be one of the team inspires loyalty and ambition among people.

This type of manager avoids confrontation; they do not want to be the bad person. They need to be accepted and they develop a false sense of security when it comes to the productivity of their people.

The walls usually come crashing down on this management style. The problem is it may take awhile for it to become known. The reason for the delay in recognizing this management style is the manager typically covers for their people. They make excuses for people and work harder to correct the situation.

The manager works harder to fill the gaps in the environment while the team figures out what they can get away with or cut corners. The end result, as we discuss later in this book, too many issues arise and the manager becomes buried in a broken environment. This is by the same people who will tell you what a great leader they think you are.

If this is you and you are beginning to realize your marshmallow approach is not working, it is time to recognize it and change. The realization typically comes in the form of increased pressure from your boss as many elements of the business fail to reach their potential. You are left holding the bag. You let this happen.

This approach lacks accountability and relies too heavily on the relationship with people. You need to understand that employees want a dividing line between a manager and their position. They need to know that someone is steering the ship and in charge.

A lack of accountability creates many morale issues as the good workers take up the slack for the bad. Can you see the exact opposite of what was intended occurring? The desire to be liked without accountability never ends well for the manager or employees.

After a manager realizes they have been under-managing the team, typically through a disciplinary process they had to endure, they feel the temptation to swing the other way. This creates other problems as they strive for over-managing, over-accountability and exclude the people connection.

The manager falsely believes that their people did this to them, the team let them down. If this is you, understand this, it is your fault. Accept responsibility and strive to make it better. The first reaction, unfortunately, is to disregard the relationship with people and begin wearing the iron fist.

You cannot transition from a marshmallow to an iron fist, nor should you. The goal is to achieve balance right down the middle. Focus on balancing accountability and relationships, suggestions are included in the following chapters.

Ruling With An Iron Fist

This type of manager is the opposing side of the spectrum; they are in charge and let employees know it (every chance they get). They rely too heavily on accountability with no connection to people.

At first blush, you might think this is the better of the two sides. At least you are getting things accomplished but your people cannot stand coming to work or the sight of you. Neither side is good to be on; they both lead to breakdowns in the human system that comprise the store environment.

This is not just a rookie mistake; I see this from experienced managers as well. They delegate everything, which is not a bad thing, but it is done with a lack of appreciation or recognition for people. They base their authority on elements of fear, a do this or else mentality. This type of managing use to fly many years ago but not today, people will not tolerate it.

It takes a while to discover this type of management style, the same as the marshmallow but for different reasons. This type of manager typically generates high turnover numbers. People have enough and they finally quit or leave the store. The manager justifies this as cleaning house or working through dead weight to get a solid team in place.

It may be true that deadweight needs to go, especially if a marshmallow managed the building prior to the new manager. The numbers will usually hit extremes and morale in the building is low. Low morale equates to low productivity.

The realization that hard work is never enough and never appreciated breeds resentment within employees. They are seen as accountable task drivers with no real connection to what they do or why they do it.

The façade falls apart as employees begin to band together with the thought of bringing the evil dictator down. They begin to file ethical complaints and to reduce their output. Absenteeism typically increases and worker compensation claims may begin to rise.

The problem with a heavy reliance on accountability and a disregard for relationships is it assumes people are like machines or robots. It becomes a mechanistic environment and does not take the human element into consideration. Employees have needs beyond knowing their job; they need a connection to make their work feel worthwhile.

The environment needs to be viewed from a humanistic perspective. There needs to be a high emphasis placed on valuing people and the work they perform. Consider the work of all of the people in a store that comprise the whole environment. Imagine what it could look like if the same people understood their role, their value to you and the organization, their actions and accountability as well as obtainable goals.

The Lighter Side - An Example

I have recently had a discussion with a new store manager of a big box retailer, Linda (A pseudo name for the manager). Her first big assignment was a store that was run well by the previous manager. The morale was stabile, sales and profits balanced and processes adequate. There seemed to be a noticeable difference in the morale in the store after she took over, for the worse.

During the discussion it became apparent that Linda was frustrated with the resistance and push back she was receiving from the staff and employees. She took the iron fist approach and entered the building with both guns blazing. The thought process was to gain respect through a dedication to getting things done.

After 3 months, a survey with employees revealed the following types of comments and attitudes. This is from their perspective.

- Linda has told us not to call her for problems.

- Linda does not speak to employees when she is on the sales floor.

- She walks by customers and does not acknowledge them but will not accept this from an employee.

- She gives direction but does not offer explanations to understand the meaning of it.

- Employees do not like her; the last manager was much more personable.

- She talks down to employees during sales floor meetings.

- No one in the store likes her, people are thinking about leaving.

I discussed the attitudes of employees with Linda and she confirmed that employees do not like her. She then said something very telling during the discussion. She said, "I think the people here are waiting to see the lighter side of me and there isn't one, they want me to laugh and be friendly but I'm not like that, I am a numbers person, I am going to wear them out."

Linda is doomed to fail. Being a numbers person is fine but you cannot manage people and hide behind that disclaimer. It takes people to generate the numbers, sales, customer service levels, control expenses, etc. She is operating in a mechanistic system and not considering the needs of the human element that is required to be successful.

The opportunity for Linda is managing down the middle. Let her experience from a financial perspective help her to connect with people. She can help them see the value or results of their work, make it more tangible. Most importantly, she needs to connect the numbers to people.

If you see glimmers of your management style that align with Linda, recognize it. Get out from behind a desk and see what transpires to achieve the numbers you place so much value in to reach goals. You need to recognize the actions required to contribute to the success or failure of the store environment. When you learn to see the store operation as a humanistic whole, you will be able to impact performance.

Chapter Two

Managing the Managers

The retail history lesson (as I see it) is now behind us and it is time to focus on the core of problem solving at the store level. My method is not a slow build from processes to people. I see the issues in stores in the opposite fashion, people to processes.

The first topic up is your management staff. Only you know or should know the true value of the people that work for you. I'm not talking about how nice they are or the amount of charity work they have done. These things are nice and you may consider them a great neighbor but I am referring to the ability and capability to perform at a high level.

Ability and capability have separate identities, though often used in the same context. Ability allows a person to be receptive and understand what they need to accomplish. In my opinion, capability refers to taking the knowledge and putting it into action. This goes beyond face value into understanding the impact of an action in the short and long-term arena. Does your management team understand the ramifications of their actions to the immediate level of the problem as well as the store and organization? Do they or you consider the store as a whole when making decisions?

Mirror Test

The answer to the above questions are typically no. You want your team to have passion for sales, you want them to make smart business decisions but we do not coach, train and educate them to act accordingly. This does not require fancy or complex philosophies. This requires accountability and an investment in development.

As a store manager, the failure of one of your management staff is comprised of your investment in the individual; this applies to the employees as well. If you are invested in the development and accountability of that individual, your conscience is clear and the job is done. If the individual received very little in the way of guidance and development from you, you are partially responsible.

I will ask you to take the mirror test several times throughout this book. The mirror test is simply this, when it comes time to document or terminate a manager, look in the mirror and ask if you have done everything to coach, train and educate that person. If the answer is yes and the individual simply does not possess the capabilities required for the job, it is time to let go. Alternatively, if you have not invested in the individual, who really failed?

The mirror test can be used in regards to your contribution to manager or employee development. It is meant to look internally at your contribution to the success of an employee or accountability in the failure of a person. Before you act or react to poor performance from a manager or employee, understand your level of support, training, coaching and development.

This does not mean you are accountable for personally and directly developing everyone in a store. You are ultimately responsible to ensure employees receive the coaching and training required to develop through their direct report.

You are the face of the store and you represent the company. Before you decide to pull the trigger and terminate someone based on performance, you need to recognize the part of your efforts that the failure represents.

What Makes This Manager A Manager?

How do you decide whom to promote or hire into a managerial position?

This is the starting point and a good indicator of your ability to choose talent. The question is how do you decide on new management talent? Chances are you are basing their potential to lead people on their performance in their current role. This person is typically the star performer in a sales or operational area or less significant managerial role.

Think about this for a second, you are saying that an individual that is a top sales person in a department will make a great manager or leader of people. This practice has to go deeper than surface abilities, what are their capabilities? Consider these points along with your interview guide:

✓What leadership qualities has this individual exhibited?

✓What barriers/ obstacles has the individual overcome?

✓What creative ideas has the individual demonstrated?

✓What level of person-to-person interaction have I witnessed with this individual?

✓What is my relationship with this person, what do I really

know?

The point is to go beyond what you know at the surface or think beyond the company script. Promoting someone based on surface information is a gamblers bet. The individual may work out well or be dead weight on the staff. There is a pretty good chance you have inherited an unproductive team member or promoted them yourself.

Look into the mirror once more, if there is dead weight on your management team, who is accountable for the current structure? If your team has unproductive members, have they been coached, trained and developed to succeed? If the answer is yes to the previous questions, what is your plan to restructure or realign talent to fit the job?

It is no mystery; if you surround yourself with a strong staff, you will unite a strong, successful team. Do not be afraid to hire or promote someone with a strength that reflects your weakness. I had a district manager tell me once that store managers should have an ego to succeed. This is not a time to let your ego get in the way of potential results.

If you wish to be the smartest in your store and this influences your hiring decisions, you are in trouble. Surround yourself with the best and brightest and develop them. Do not be intimidated by someone with more experience, leverage their experience to drive results, they win, YOU WIN.

Accountability: Through or Around?

This may seem like a strange segment but let me assure you that I have seen very talented managers brought down by managing around their managers. The marshmallow manager is in full swing when it involves lack of accountability and managing through people.

Managing around your managers means that you do not utilize your team to get things accomplished. In an effort to get your arms around everything and share the workload, you take on all of the workload via creating plans and delegating to lower level managers. This occurs in a few different scenarios from a new manager, considering yourself one of the team and managing around weak performers.

These are examples of the extremes mentioned in Chapter One but they are surprisingly common. They result from an imbalance in accountability and people related skills. The existence of one or the other lacks the appropriate measure, which results in an out of balance approach.

The difficult part, at times, is finding the middle of the road to create balance. The first step is recognition of existing behaviors that contribute to an ineffective environment. There are many signs that will typically point in this direction. If your boss is dissecting your business on a consistent basis and you walk away with 10 pages of notes each time you need to look within for change.

If all signs are pointing to problem, there is one. Another good indicator for store managers is their inability to get things done while their staff has little to do; you are managing around your managers. Your slate should be clean of things to do, through delegation. Your list exists for checks and balances. In other words, to ensure your team has completed what they were asked to do. If you are, doing all of the heavy lifting the tail may be wagging the dog.

First - New Manager

First, new managers tend to manage around managers. The new manager places an extreme importance on assimilation and acceptance. This comes mainly from inexperience and is a way for the manager to show they are part of the team and they understand or value their management team. This is a big mistake and ends in the exact opposite result of what was anticipated. This does not mean a new manager has to enter a building, running well or broken, with both guns blazing. If you do not start by managing through your management team, it will be difficult to do later.

Managing through your team equals accountability and successful delegation. Managing through your management staff requires that you clarify their roles, set parameters, detail accountability and expectations. This does not require a blazing guns approach, rather, an understanding of what you expect. The most important piece to this approach is to represent the value of your expectations. How will it support customer service initiatives and their career?

This is much better handled on two separate levels. First, meet as a team and then individually. There is a flow to getting yourself and ideals acquainted with the team. The following represents more of a flow than checklist.

✓Try to get all of the senior level managers together for the first meeting. Consider this an introduction, tell them briefly about you and learn basic information about them. If this is your first assignment with the company, it will require a more in depth discussion. More than likely you have worked for the company in some capacity. Keep the meeting brief.

✓Print and distribute a copy of the organizations' mission statement or vision. This will probably be the first time your team, possibly you, ever read the statement. This is the gauge of all activities and tasks including customer service levels in the future. Anything that does not align with the mission or vision is unproductive. The goal of the store team is to assist the organization with achieving its goals. This is a great starting point to align your expectations and behaviors with the organization.

✓Discuss your experiences both good and bad to this

point in the company. Ask the team for their input on what is going well and where they feel improvement is needed in their assigned areas.

✓Discuss customer service expectations and team driven goals. The key word is discuss which means an open forum. Nobody wants to hear your philosophies for hours, it is boring and it makes the statement that your ideas are the best and you are not open to any other collaboration. If you want a team environment, it begins here. Keep the meeting short and sweet, the next phase is meeting one on one through the next week.

✓Discuss your plan to meet one on one to gain insight into their roles, the people and processes they manage, customer service levels, their aspirations and their ideas and suggestions. They should come prepared for the short sessions to discuss these issues as well as succession planning for the leaders and key players on their team. During these short sessions, you should discuss your expectations of the position including how you lead people. Commit to their personal development through coaching, training, accountability, honest feedback and collaboration.

✓Finally, ask for their commitment to the store, its people and the organization. I have done this many times and it is a much better way to strengthen the relationship and begin gauging the commitment level of your team than drowning them in philosophies.

Second - One of the Team

The second issue to address in managing around your managers is the desire to be one of the team.

Whether you believe it or not, there has to be a difference between the team and the leader. You cannot act as if you are on the same level as your team; they need to know there is a line. I understand the desire to not differentiate yourself from your managers. There is a feeling that the team will appreciate your "in the trenches" mentality and will work harder for your efforts. This thought process is flawed.

Your team needs a leader as well as direction and structure. If there is not a clear decision maker at the top, the team environment will collapse. Listen to me as I have learned through experience, it is great to appreciate your team and value their efforts but you cannot blur the line in the relationship. This will ultimately end in damaging the relationship.

This is not to say that you should be cold, abrasive and not get to know your team and their lives. If you follow the direction in setting up the initial and one on one meeting you will set the tone for the relationship.

Here are a few points to avoid being trapped in "one of the team" managerial mistakes.

✓Avoid gossip, both listening and contributing.

✓Understand the words you say WILL be repeated. No matter how trustworthy you feel the source is, confide cautiously. The human resource manager should be a genuine source of trust but the title does not guarantee it. You may be unaware of the relationship this person has with other managers or employees. If you are expressing an opinion, it may get back to that individual. I cannot tell you how many conversations among the ranks start with "Do not repeat this…" or "You never heard this from me…"

✓Guard your words and actions. You cannot use language or tell stories to your management staff as if you were one of them. Yes, you are a team player but you are held to a higher level of behavior. For example, telling a joke that contains language or thoughts that may offend someone may not seem like a big deal right now, until you have to discipline a manager for behavior that you are guilty of yourself.

How do you discipline or terminate someone over words or actions that you are personally guilty of engaging in? Do you feel the room getting smaller now? You should, if your behaviors are unprofessional, no one and I mean no one will come to your defense when you are in the hot seat. If you have crossed the line, no one can save your job or the damage to trust and morale.

✓Avoid socializing, this is another guard your words and actions moment. Unless it is a business function, socializing with members of the team creates animosity. If you go to lunch with the same manager everyday you are creating tension within the ranks and worst of all feelings of mistrust. You are essentially killing morale. You may have been friends for twenty years prior to your assignment but now you are viewed as the leader with the necessity to treat people fairly.

For example, I worked for a male store manager that recently promoted a female manager in the store. Uncharacteristically, he took her to lunch several times per week. He saw it as time to share thoughts and develop her managerial skills. Big problem, he never went to lunch with anyone else, it was not long before jealously led to accusations of an affair among the team. Trust was broken. Even though the manager's intention of coaching and training were good, his actions were not.

GUARD YOUR WORDS AND ACTIONS! If you are going to have lunch with managers, ensure you include everyone at some point. Everyone wants your time and attention, even those that admittedly do not like you; want face time with the boss.

✓Review and understand your organizations policies on Zero Tolerance, most organizations have them. Better yet, review the consequences for unprofessional actions, most end in termination. Do not believe me, read the policies, learn them and live them. In lawsuit happy America, not one organization is going to give you a second chance to cost them millions defending careless actions.

✓Finally, do not create exceptions to policies. If your policy states that you are to report misconduct of a manager or employee that was brought to you, do it. I have many stories about the "best managers" being terminated for stupid behavior. Policies must be followed, if you overlook or do not report something because of the perceived performance level of a manager, you very well may be gone if the action is discovered.

Whew! It sure is lonely at the top, isn't it? Some would say it is no fun. Success and wins should be fun and celebrated without crossing a line. It is ok to get excited and make some noise over a big win, just remember this is not your backyard, your actions and words are on display.

You should get to know your managers, about their lives, if they have kids, where they went on vacation, maybe a good book they have read.

You need to be personable to relate to people, just guard your words and actions. You can interact and show your personality without crossing a line. If you do not say or do anything you need to worry about, you will not need to worry. If you are frustrated or upset, temper your reaction in front of others. You can go to your car, by yourself, and scream every curse word that makes you feel better, just not in front of the staff. It is good to be direct with the team if there is an issue, it is ok to show emotion, just do not go overboard.

Third - Managing Around Weak Performers

I have personally witnessed many managers fail by managing around managers, especially weak performers. Please do not tell me that you do not know who the weak players are, just as well as you know, so does your staff. Your staff is left to clean up after this person and ultimately you are protecting or avoiding someone who will leave you holding the proverbial bag.

My point, you know who the weak performers are, right? If not, you should know this and I'm sure most on your staff will be quick to identify them. If you think managing around them is a good idea, please rethink your strategy.

I know it is difficult in large organizations to terminate an employee based on performance. I side with the company on this one. Managers are so inconsistent across a retail chain of handling, documenting and addressing poor performers that a valid case is hard to move on for fear of being sued. Do you blame them? If you have managed for a while, you know what I am talking about; you may be guilty of this.

Here is typically how the story goes. Let's say Bob is your weakest performer on the management staff. What makes Bob so ineffective? He does not get work done in his area on a regular basis, which creates a heavier workload for others, he does not hold his team accountable, and he is disorganized and really works hard but accomplishes nothing.

You are aware of Bob's shortcomings and will be sure to address them on his annual review ten months from now. Until then, you will continue to pile the work on the strong performers and feel good that you have made a great managerial decision to give the work to a manager that will get the job done.

Your behavior is saying, the more inept that you are, the less of a workload you will get. Do you think your top performers enjoy watching this transpire right in front of them? Of course, they are going to smile and nod their head yes to everything but slowly resentment builds. You are once again killing your morale and you won't even see it happening.

STOP this cycle, identify your weak performers and pull out your magic mirror again. Think about the specifics of what is making them ineffective. Look in the mirror and ask, "Did this individual get here on their own?" If you have not been directly involved with coaching, training and developing the manager, who has failed? These issues must be dealt with directly, continuing to work around the manager leads to this question, who is accountable?

Deal with the weak performer(s) through coaching, training and developing their skills, more on this topic in the next segment. The goal is to improve performance, not to see them fail. This can be accomplished by pairing managers to leverage strengths and create a tighter team bond among the ranks. Your top performers will still view the partner method as a task but they understand the success of the partner is a reflection on their level of talent.

You must develop an action plan for improvement as a collaborative effort. I know that everyone is action planned to death. They are the cure all for everything, write a plan and the individual or situation magically improves. Not true but a necessity as a document to show your efforts. Follow your organizations Human Resource policies for documenting performance improvement. The heart of the plan must consist of:

✓Specific problems and specific solutions, no generalities. If it comes down to terminating or removing the individual, generalities will not cut it at the corporate HR level.

✓Timelines, deadlines, follow up and milestones must be noted. Plans are useless without documenting when the improvement should be noticed and when you will follow up to review progress. There should not be a long period of time between progress reviews, 30 days at the most. Beyond 30 does not reflect the willingness to assist with improvement and allows sub-par behavior to continue.

✓Facts, keep your personal feelings out of it. Everything you document should be fact, not emotion. You may not personally like this individual. Chances are, you have become angry or irritated over their performance, and maybe another mirror test may be required. You should want everyone on your team to succeed, if the team wins than you win.

✓What you expect, the plan for improvement. Be sure the plan is realistic and comparable to what you would ask from the rest of the staff in terms of workload. The exception would be a unique position that requires a more detailed workload.

You must include how the individual can seek help, if needed. How do they ask for help? Should they schedule a meeting, make a request via email, meet with you briefly each week to update you on progress and ask for recommendations (highly recommended). This puts the onus on that person to improve.

If they are still drowning at the end of the process, it is documented that you offered unlimited assistance to improve. More importantly, the additional guidance may help them improve which will strengthen your team and morale among managers.

✓The consequences for not improving must be documented. This is where documenting your plan to help the manager from the last step, will come in handy. The individual must be clear of what will happen or be considered if they do not improve. Place an emphasis on the value of their improved state, what would it represent to the team?

Chapter Three
Employee Morale

Let's turn our attention to a universal matter for all managers. Regardless of your managerial role, the productive nature and commitment level of your employees is dependent upon their satisfaction in their roles. Do not underestimate the power of a positive work environment. We have discussed a lot about accountability. Please be clear that a positive work environment does not excuse bad behavior. A positive morale will contribute to productive work that aligns with the organization's vision.

Too often managers fail to recognize the good behaviors demonstrated by their people, it is much easier to manage by exception. For most major retail chains there are a million reports that examine every angle of performance. There are sales reports, margin, expense, payroll, credit acquisition, employee sales, miscellaneous income such as extended warranties, training, returns, leads, etc. The list will go on and on, some reports are heavily relied on, while others that contain important information are never used. There are only so many hours in the day and I'm not here to tell you what is important to your boss, you already know.

Employee morale and development are a vicious cycle, it seems you need a good morale to have a learning environment or does a learning environment contribute to improving morale? I tend to believe that morale must be in good shape or being repaired for employees to want to develop and learn.

This will never mean that every employee is smiling while walking into work every day and fulfill everything they are asked to do. This means that employees are treated fairly, with respect, clearly defined goals, they understand how their work contributes to the store and organizations vision and offered honest feedback and support.

In most cases, there is a pay range assigned to job codes and you may not have any say or consideration in this area. Do not focus on it, if the individual accepted the position they are committing to doing the job.

Get Your Morale In-Check

The first step in determining your current morale is from the employee level. Do not take your senior level managers word for the current state of the store environment. They are, at times, isolated from the real problems or may refuse to clearly see the issues.

If you are an experienced manager, you may pick up on the store "vibe" immediately. If not, your company may have an employee opinion survey they conduct every year or two years, review these results as a starting point.

Typically, department level managers are in-tune with morale as employees see them as on their side and confide in them. A department level manger is usually very defensive of their people, which generate a stronger bond between them.

Basically, they are "in the know" if people are satisfied or there are numerous complaints. Start with your department level mangers to gain insight and awareness to some of the issues. These managers are less likely to manage through reporting and more apt to really know their people.

As a new manager to the role or store, regardless of the level, the best place to start is by working along side your people and discussing their view. This is not meant to be an unrealistic complaint session such as a new computer system or rearranging the store. This should focus on what is right and wrong within the current structure.

Simply ask how they feel about their job and notice ongoing themes. If you are speaking with the 20th employee and they have all recognized communication as a major issue, there is a good chance that an issue exists. Be very cautious, if you speak with 49/50 employees, the one you missed may feel they are not important.

Speaking with every employee may not be a reality within a short window. Begin the process and take it slow (with urgency) to digest the information. Ensure you have created time lines. Utilize morning, afternoon or evening meetings that most retailers require to begin changing the culture through recognition of the positive accomplishments. Treat the opportunity areas as educational and do not single out performers negatively. This is the opportunity to begin building both a positive and educational culture.

Building and Sustaining a Winning Culture

There are dozens of books and articles from human resources professionals that discuss the significance of culture. This goes beyond a diverse mix of people and your organizations efforts to balance the workforce in ethnic terms. I'll let those books discuss the interrelationship aspects of culture and we will talk life in the trenches.

OK, this has to be more than a slogan and more than a

corporate poster on the training room wall. Call it what you want; a winning culture, positive environment, outstanding morale or valuing diversity. The point is that you, the manager, is in tune with the environment and understand its importance to the stores' success. Understanding the current state of morale reflects your level of valuing your people.

I have worked for several different companies, large and small. The one thing that drives me insane is company-wide meetings where the big dogs get up in front of a room full of people, potentially thousands, and tell you how important you are and how that should translate from you to your people.

The reason for my discomfort in this is the obvious disconnect between corporate philosophy and reality. Basically, the ivory tower never touches the ground. The senior organizational leaders assume what is expressed is lived. The problem is all of the variables in between.

The variables are layers of managers topped with the pressures of maintaining a store that is analyzed by 100 separate reports. Just because the top brass states you are appreciated does not mean your immediate manager, saddled with her own pressures, will take this meaning the same. What occurs, in turn, is another interpretation at the store level. The management team values people at varied levels.

What all of this means is simply VALUE your people. This is not as easy as it sounds for some managers. I do not care what the top brass says and how that may not parlay to you being treated fairly and with respect. You need to appreciate the work of the employees working hard for you. There is also a need to be sensitive to dispersing the workload and holding individuals accountable.

Show Me the Value

The key to creating lasting change is getting your staff to understand the value in what they do. They need to know that going the extra mile is recognized and appreciated to want to give the effort. They need to know how the work they perform gets the organization closer to the vision. What value do they represent to the organization and you?

The best route to begin building a better morale is recognition. This does not have to be awards or monetary prizes. In most cases, publically or privately acknowledging a great performance goes a long way. You need to know your people and how they prefer to be recognized, some are quiet and one-on-one acknowledgement will suffice while others like to bask in the spotlight.

Make a big deal of even small wins. People love to be recognized. It must be sincere and not done off of a checklist, do it because you appreciate the little and big wins.

Do not make every celebration about sales performance. This alienates the non-selling roles. It could be something such as the truck-unload team has zero damages for the last month or the efforts of an employee cleaning restrooms or break rooms. The obvious sales stuff should be celebrated, of course, but catch your team doing other things right that impact the customer experience.

Chances are your organization has an employee of the month program. You know the one; the joke among the employees of who hasn't received it yet will get it this month. This typically comes with a lame certificate and even lamer photo of the employee with a manager. These programs are so watered down; they do not mean what you think they do. I'm not saying that an employee does not appreciate being recognized but it is truly a "who's next" award as opposed to something with real meaning.

Make it a real connection experience. Recognize the individual for specific contributions. Humanize this program. Tell a story of how you caught them doing something right; share a customer feedback letter or email. Make it personal and make it consistent. Do not go overboard. Be genuine and sincere.

If you view the efforts of your people as just a part of their job, you are in for a rough road. They can get substandard management with no recognition anywhere. Make your place different.

Managerial Morale

The morale of managers in a store plays a significant part in the make-up of the environment. It is often thought to value employees, while working managers to death. This managerial beat down is accepted because managers accept a higher level of responsibility and may want to rise through the ranks.

If you base your handling of managers on these ridiculous notions, it will result in overworked managers with a disregard for your efforts. They will respect the title but not the person. They will work hard with one foot out the door, they will look for other internal opportunities or leave the company.

Managers deserve the same respect as employees. This does not mean their workload or accountability is lighter. Morale can be improved throughout your managerial ranks. Recognize them for individual and team performance. This should be more of a one-on one conversation. These conversations should be frequent and kept separate from other issues. The goal is to gain further buy-in and commitment to the organization's vision through recognition of the efforts to achieve it.

A positive morale is required for managers to be accepting of development efforts. Do not assume your managers will work harder in a tougher environment. Ruling with an iron fist does not guarantee results or forward progress.

Ensuring you have the right environment for development and accountability is a key to forward progress. Consider educating your staff through coaching, training and development to achieve goals as opposed to demanding they achieve goals they are not equipped to reach.

Chapter Four

Development

We have discussed employee morale; it is a difficult subject to pin down with so many environments and variables to consider. I believe morale must be on its way to repair to begin focusing on employee development.

Morale will never be perfect but there is a big difference in the "feel" between stores that have a solid morale and stores that have an opportunity. You can sense the difference the moment you enter the building. Employee development contributes to that solid environment, reduces turnover and attracts talent.

A colleague and former supervisor of mine, Wayne, understood the value of development. He suggested that it is better to invest time into development to enable a greater chance of success than risk a greater chance of failure in the current state. I agree with this notion, an investment in development moves the team in unison towards the vision.

This can be a daunting task; stages of employee development are not as noticeable on the surface as morale. In fact, it may be noticed by your customers before you realize there is a deficiency. You may become aware of the need for employee engagement and development through customer complaints to your store or a corporate complaint hotline.

Before we get too deep into this topic, let's discuss its reality. The need for employee development is not exclusive for those working to transition into management. Employee development is universal throughout the store regardless of future aspirations. The accountability of developing the employee team lies directly on managers.

The store manager has double duty. They are accountable for employee and management staff development. At times, these are one and the same. The ability of the store manager to develop their managers will provide the necessary tools for them to develop their employees.

Coach, Train & Develop - Managers

This segment is as important as it is overlooked. I have mentioned coaching, training and developing managers a few times throughout the text. This is a store manager's accountability. This is not to say a store manager is responsible for every aspect of development but they are responsible for ensuring a manager is developing in their role. This is an ongoing requirement and not once or twice a year during a review process.

This can be double duty for all layers of management. You have to develop your managers to improve or sharpen skills and you have to teach them how to develop their people. You are killing two birds with one stone, or is it a heavy rock? Either way, this task takes planning and structure, off the cuff will give you mediocre results.

First, you need to assess the current state of your management staff, whether you are a store manager and evaluating the senior managers or part of the management staff with department managers that report to you. You need this assessment to have a starting point and identify their strengths and weaknesses. You can utilize previous annual reviews to gain insight into their opportunities and any documentation in their file to identify behaviors.

Next, review any recent reporting or audits that serve as a report card for effectiveness. This can be done with the help of human resources to gain their perspective and include them as a part of the management staff. This assessment should include a managers' entire area of responsibility.

If the individual is responsible for non-selling functions for example, you will need reporting that shows all of their accountability areas, this will help with efforts to improve their leadership skills. Finally, note any personal observations both good and bad of the individuals' performance.

The next step is time consuming but necessary. You need to have a one-on-one conversation with the manager. This should not wait until an annual review and there should be no distractions. If you begin a conversation and you are answering your store phone or cell phone every five minutes, how committed are you? How committed do you think a manager will be to the assessment?

The following are some general guidelines for the conversation:

✓Discuss the data or hard facts about their area of responsibility. Do not discuss personal observations yet.

✓Let the manager discuss their performance. Be aware of the difference between roadblocks and excuses. A roadblock is a legitimate universal barrier to success with attempts to overcome it. For example, sales have struggled due to a lack of inventory experienced company-wide. They have increased quantities on substitute items and the department manager has been coached to overcome objections. An excuse for the same issue, the company has screwed us with inventory; there is nothing we can do.

✓Ask them to discuss their personal interaction and engagement with customers and their employees.

✓Now you can constructively discuss your observations both good and bad. Maybe the manager is excellent with customers but lacks planning and accountability with their people.

✓Ask the manager to rate their effectiveness from 1 to 5 (5 being the best) in the following areas (you can add or take away areas; this is to give you insight into their perception of current skills):

- Customer service
- Employee development (coaching, training)
- Follow-up/ feedback to employees (this would include tasks, sales numbers, constructive criticism)
- Delegation
- Planning
- Problem solving (are they using tools such as reporting to identify problem areas)
- Competition (comparing their area's performance against nearby stores and competitors)
- How do they think their team would rate them?

✓Discuss their effectiveness ratings, elaborate on their meaning and where you see the value of the team and the managers' contributions (you do not need to counter their assessment number with a number, the point is to be educational, not confrontational).

✓How will the manager improve? Discuss details and deadlines.

✓Ask for a commitment to the organizations vision.

✓Ensure you set a follow up meeting to briefly discuss progress and your continued observations.

I know these suggestions seem generic; it is very difficult to create a specific action plan to fit every situation. The goal is to gain an understanding of your staff's capabilities with this exercise. You need to determine what they require to enable growth in their position.

The most lacking detail is accountability and delegation. I explained in chapter two the different scenarios that lead to poor accountability. You need to develop your staff through accountability measures. They need to understand their business area and how it impacts the entire store. You need to challenge them on learning everything about their business.

For your manager, senior level or department, to develop you must hold them accountable for knowing and understanding at a deep level:

✓Policies and procedures.

✓Organizational vision and values.

✓The strengths and weaknesses of their team members/ the performance of their individual employees (this will help them identify employees that need coaching and training).

✓Succession planning.

✓The sales and profit performance of their area of responsibility and the entire store (they need to understand how change in their area impacts the store as a whole).

✓Customers, if the business is a customer relationship-building business such as business-to-business sales, do the manager and team know their customers. This goes beyond seeing the customer in the store, do they know buying trends, projects and are they able to anticipate needs.

✓Merchandising and recovery standards.

✓Competition.

✓Short term and long term planning.

This is again a short and varied list; the point is not the content of this list but the insistence that managers are held accountable. I believe accountability drives development. If your managers are personally involved in the growth of their people and business, they will clearly understand the components that comprise the whole.

You must schedule time to meet with your managers on a regular basis to review their areas of accountability. This does not need to be formal, it can occur during your daily rounds.

The manager should possess the ability to review their business quickly and concisely. Challenge your managers on the list of knowledge and understanding items that you have created, the challenge will assist in their development.

Coach, Train & Develop - Employees

The reason we started with discussing managerial development is the direct influence your management team has over the employee teams. If your manager is not developing or they do not recognize a good structure through your interaction and example, they will not develop their team.

The right environment for growing and learning requires a mixture of positive energy, clear understanding of an employees' role and expectations and supportive managerial interaction.

Your employees need to understand their contribution to the team and level of accountability. The first step here is similar to your management staff. You need to assess their current state. This is impossible for a single manager or store manager to complete. You need to rely on the judgment of the management staff.

If you started with the previous step of developing your managers and instructing them on the value of coaching, training and development, it should be readily accepted and practiced. If you are assuming the current state of the environment encourages growth, you may be mistaken.

Much like the previous manager lists, your employees need to understand the depth of their position. They need to know where they fit into the big picture and morale must be stabile or on its way to being repaired to a higher state. Most organizations have an annual review process that tells half of the story. There is a good portion of your management staff that has no idea how to evaluate the skill set and necessary developmental needs of an employee.

Most review processes are one-way conversations, the managers states what they think, they label the individual with a number and they place a checkmark on a sheet that indicates the review is completed.

My favorite part of a review is when the manager states that no one gets a top score because there is always room to grow. There always will be room to grow but don't count on the manager to help the employee get there, in most cases the employee is on their own.

If you indicate a room for growth, what is it, where is it and how does the employee improve? If you can't answer these questions, how do you expect your employees to answer them or care about improving?

The employees need to be developed through positive reinforcement and accountability. You need to acknowledge the things they do right. This is a big fear for managers, if they tell an employee they have done a great job will the employee continue to work as hard. This notion is off base, an employee needs to be told the good things to reinforce value in their efforts and position.

In big retailers, an employee can feel their contribution is meaningless. If you are not recognizing the good, you are missing a huge opportunity to improve morale and team motivation.

The recognition of doing something right goes further than a monetary reward. Everyone wants to feel good about their accomplishments. The acknowledgment must be specific in nature, no generalities. The recognition must remain pure. Pure recognition is stating what the individual has done well and not adding on to it.

It is infuriating to hear a manager call out an employee in a meeting or huddle and state what they have down well and destroy it with their own special brand of motivation. For example, Jane opened up the most credit accounts yesterday, that's awesome….wait for it and here it comes...Jane, we need you give us double that today…managerial magic. You have built someone up only to crush them. Keep the recognition pure; do not add to it, here is a brief list of do's and don'ts.

✓<u>Do not</u> recognize and coach in the same breath. Offer recognition and wait until another time to discuss a coaching issue.

✓<u>Do not</u> offer recognition with a new goal attached. The goal is to appreciate an effort not offer more pressure in the form of "now, give me more".

✓<u>Do</u> speak from the heart, be sincere and be interested.

✓<u>Do</u> the recognition in front of a group where possible.

✓<u>Do</u> the recognition in a timely manner. Highlighting an effort from two months ago will not get the team motivated or have an impact on the individual.

Recognition is only one important piece of the puzzle. Accountability is huge. There are a lot of managers that jump to negative thoughts on the topic of accountability. They assume accountability implies discipline. This thought is incorrect. Accountability should be viewed as an employee that has a clear understanding of their role and expectations. If you have done your job and defined the roles of employees, how they represent value and aligned their work with the organization's vision, they should know where their accountability lies.

A mirror test is in order here. If you can look in the mirror and ask yourself about employee accountability and you come up with an unclear vision and unsettled feeling, you may not have done everything you can to get this right.

This segment of the book is not meant to offer an exhaustive look at development; rather, it is intended to stimulate thought and reflection around this topic.

Guard Your Words & Actions

Part of developing managers and employees is having inspirational and confrontational encounters. These interactions may vary widely but they contain one constant variable that must be adhered to. Regardless of the situation or circumstance there must be an effort to temper your reaction.

This becomes difficult in highly stressful situations. I have witnessed displays with managers that were completely irate, out of control and using every word in the profanity dictionary and creating a few of their own. This is not a great situation to be in.

Higher-level managers feel comfortable throwing around curse words as a show of aggressive behavior and to represent power. They feel that anything they dish out must be absorbed by lower tiered managers. They use casual language and actions to represent the forceful nature of the message. For example, slamming your fist on the desk and screaming expletives at someone to get something done.

Keep in mind that unprofessional behaviors are typically defined by HR managers in large organizations. They are printed in policy form to protect the company and employees from undesirable behavior and actions. You should know and understand these policies.

Some retailers have Zero Tolerance policies when it comes to undesirable actions such as profanity, racially and ethnically charged discussions or jokes, sexual conversations or overtures, socializing with employees for non-business functions, aggressive actions or public displays to embarrass employees, etc.

These policies are key to maintain a productive work environment and to keep lawsuits from occurring. Organizations are aware of the cost involved with defending careless actions in court. In a great number of incidents, there is no second chance. Keep that in mind when you think about the way you interact with people.

Guarding your words and actions is not a situation-by-situation consideration, it is an all day, all the time standard. It refers to acting professionally regardless of the situation or your personal thermostat. I referenced guarding your words and actions in Chapter Two but I feel it necessary to expand further.

Guarding your words and actions is leading by example. Managers put themselves in a tough situation when they exhibit behaviors that break policies and have to discipline others for the same offense. It is an impossible situation.

Employees know unacceptable behavior when they see it. You may be a highly revered manager that has been with the company exhibiting the same behavior for 30 years. The problem is this, all that it takes is 1 person to be offended by your actions and report them to get the ball rolling.

You will find no support when you are in the hot seat, employees and colleagues will distance themselves. If your company has a Zero Tolerance Policy, no amount of friendships will save you. You are not above policy, especially HR policies.

This applies to non-business social situations as well. If you socialize with your employees or managers that report to you, you are severely diminishing your managing abilities. There has to be a line drawn between the manager and employee relationship. When the line is crossed, you leave yourself open to an employee or manager's interpretation of your actions. If you do something offensive during a social gathering, it can impact the working relationship.

Bottom line, do not do or say anything that leaves you unprotected. Remember to guard your words and actions and you will not need to worry about something blowing up on you. This does mean you have to sugar coat everything or not be personable, just understand where to draw the line.

Chapter Five
The Blind Defender

The title of this chapter may surprise you, everything to this point has been about improving the environment, managers and employees. We will now focus on recognizing problems within the store. This segment aligns with managing around managers in many ways. Let's begin with a story that illustrates this chapter well.

I was a part of conference call with a district manager, area business manager and store manager, James (a pseudo name for the store manager). The goal of the call was to examine a few specific business functions in the store. The district manager was discussing problems that he saw from a productivity standpoint via reporting. The area manager chimed in and spoke of organizational issues with paperwork and customer follow up.

James was not receptive to outside opinions of the business. He saw this as an attack on his personal skills. He refused to agree with the observations and finally stated that he just does not see what others were observing. After numerous attempts to show him that potential problems exist, James continued to blindly defend the actions of his people.

He was arguing against the facts, this is when you know you have crossed the line from rational understanding to a blind defender. The tail has begun to wag the dog.

Stop Defending Your Team

The blind defender is a manager, at any level, that cannot see the reality of productivity and results within their environment. They blindly believe that everything their team does comes from hard work, in the best interest of the business, is at their full potential and must be at a high level. They believe their leadership instills a hard working spirit within their employees. If they protect their people, their people will work hard for them.

I have seen this a million times, it is easy to believe everyone will do their best based on their own motivation and initiative. I have fallen prey to this as well. There was a time that I managed many different areas within a big box store. One of those areas consisted of a business-to-business sales area. Here is an example of a typical blind defender story.

I would ask if the team was going to meet their weekly budget (not a great example of accountability or development, is it?). They would tell me stories of great sales that were coming our way, some worth $10 or $15k. They told me how hard they were working to get sales, near exhaustion. They were pulling all of the stops, gathering all of their strength to combat the competition to win. Sounds dramatic, but that is the way I believed it.

As weeks would go by, occasionally one of the wins would come through but most never materialized. When I continually inquired about the pending dream sales we were waiting for, the team had other explanations. They blamed everyone and everything and continued to explain that their efforts went above and beyond. In the end, there was no one that could have done anything else to capture the sale. They believed it and so did I, for a while.

I believed in them blindly, even when the numbers and stories did not add up, it was easier to believe than challenge and create accountable measures. Besides, there were so many other things to do and if I admitted to others and myself the team was not performing at the perceived level I would have to address it.

When others would question the ability and capability of the team in regards to tangible results, I defended them. I told my superiors about their hard work, good intentions, and high level of skill and material knowledge.

The blind defense was perpetuated as my supervisors blindly believed the teams unwavering efforts. There was no reason for them not to believe, it was a similar situation in many of the stores in that market. Many managers did not understand the application of the material and chose to manage from a distance.

Lazy or Not Focused

Lazy or not focused, in my example above, where did I fall between these two choices? Maybe I made excuses and it was just easier to blindly defend than fix the situation, lazy? Maybe I was not focused on the components of the business, from a detailed or big picture view, not focused?

At first, I believed that a blind defender was a lazy manager. They did not want to realize an area of opportunity because the thought of discovery, planning, implementing and developing the team seems monumental. There are so many pressing issues that require attention, that this issue takes a back seat.

My opinion slowly changed after analyzing the situation. Managers are not typically lazy, they are pulled in many directions. There are not enough hours in the day to get everything done. I believe they let non-productive work get in the way of aligning the team efforts with the vision. They look the other way out of a lack of focus on development and accountability.

The lack of focus is allowed to exist through the avoidance of validation. In essence, focus requires digging beneath the surface to determine the mechanics of a team or effort. Laziness would avoid the validation process in an effort to clear the slate, to have nothing left to do. A lack of focus is validation avoidance in an effort to concentrate on something else.

This is where coaching, training and developing managers is crucial. A manager that is unfocused willingly accepts surface results as an effort to get their arms around as many things as possible. They have a hard time prioritizing; they do not delegate responsibility or have accountability measures. They believe what they are told without consideration of the experience, knowledge or factual data the source possesses.

The Tail Wags The Dog

I'm sure you have heard of this expression at some point during your career. The tail wags the dog aligns with this chapter well. Another popular expression is the inmates are running the prison. Either way they both represent a loss of control on the part of managers. The employees are dictating what happens next. The dog should be in control of the tail, not at the mercy of it.

Managers should be in control of their buildings, both people and processes. Becoming a blind defender is one way of allowing employees to tell you what they will and will not do. When a behavior or attitude is present in the store, you have allowed it to be there. Ignoring or avoiding it will not make it go away.

Managing around managers and employees is another way that represents a loss of control, as we discussed in Chapter Two. In any scenario, a loss of control will never end in a manager's favor. The loss will gain momentum and spread to other areas. It is like a wild fire, hard to contain once it has begun.

Hung Out to Dry

Make your environment and success a choice, not a time bomb waiting to explode. The problem with blinders is that you never really know what is going on behind the scenes. You are not in touch.

Defending your people is right in the proper context. A manager should be proud of their team and defend their working conditions and unfair treatment. They should ensure their people have the same opportunities as other stores to make a fair wage and have advancement and bonus opportunities. These are admiral defenses for the betterment of your people.

What we are discussing is blindly defending the productivity and progress of your team. If this feels like your flying too managerially low, you need to consider the impact on employees of turnover, poor customer service, poor morale as well as productivity that does not align with the vision.

You need to understand that your blind devotion to your team will not be reciprocated. It is human nature to do the least as possible. When your employees figure out where they can cut corners, because no one is looking, customer service will be sacrificed.

At the end of the day, when you are in a position to have to answer for all of the shortcomings of your team, no one is going to stand up for you. Not that it would matter; a manager is accountable for the performance of the team. No one can help you if you are not in control. You will be on the hook for a lack of structure; you will be hung out to dry and rightfully so.

See the Light

It is time to take off the blinders. If all business indicators point to a problem, there is a good chance, there is one. We have discussed valuing and appreciating your people. They need to be coached, trained and developed.

Evaluate their performance from a developmental and accountability perspective. If you continue to ignore the red flags, the situation will take you down. You will find yourself out of a job, still defending your people with no clue it was your fault. I'm here to tell you it is.

Accept the responsibility and blame and only then, you will be able to change. Trust me when I tell you, after assessing your environment and developing your managers and employees, the morale of the building and success of the business will greatly improve.

Take out the mirror and assess your culpability in the unproductive or excuse driven status of your store. The great news is that you can fix this through determination and development of your people, not easy but it definitely can be done.

Please be sure of compliancy with policies and procedures. These are already established, they cannot be easily changed so do not try. Most of the established policies are installed to create a structured and fair work environment.

Leverage established policies to ensure fair treatment with employees and as accountability measures. If you have done everything to try and develop an employee there is a next step, turn no further than your HR policies for the answer and guidance throughout the process. Know these policies to ensure compliancy throughout any disciplinary processes.

Chapter Six
The Demanding Customer & Competition

Have you ever thought that retail life would be so easy, except for the customers? I am sure you have when you are recovering the store standards at night or just received an earful from a customer. Another time this may creep into your mind is experiencing a sales decline or the opening of a competitor down the street.

I know you self-correct and state how important the customer is to your store. You eventually succumb to the old standard of, without customers, you would not have a job line of thinking. This thought is correct but it does not make it any easier to deal with the tough days. Rest assured the competitor down the street is experiencing the same thing.

The recession and Internet has brought about a tough, well-informed breed of customer. It is now simple to shop the competition from your phone while you are standing in a retail store. Customers are more retail educated than ever before. Not only are you competing against the brick and mortar store down the street but the entire Internet as well.

We will take these issues, customers and competition, separately though they share commonalities. These two areas are a great example of an opportunity to shift from frustration to exhilaration. The opportunities are in your building everyday but the environment must be conducive to it. You must have a positive morale or a repair in progress and the vision must be lived via development and accountability to be successful here.

These Customers Are Driving Me Crazy

The title says it all; you would be able to get a lot done every day if it was not for the demanding customers. There is no doubt that customers understand the position of power they are in and they leverage it. The power was heightened during the recession as retailers fought over every dollar. This mentality will continue going forward.

Customers understand their options and that customer services have expanded to include even the most ridiculous circumstances. All of the tension and battles over wallet share means your customer must have a quality experience in your store.

Most retailers offer guidelines to customer service in their employee-training program. They also include the customer in their vision statement and develop employee programs and incentives around a high level of service. This is another case of because it is spoken, it must be happening.

Customer service has to be more than a slogan. It is easy to be insincere and hide behind the company motto of outstanding customer service while you walk by customers on the sales floor without saying a word. Some of the best managers I have known were not afraid of customers; they were boisterous, outgoing and connected with people.

No one is perfect, even the best managers are irritated at some point with a customer. These managers did not avoid aisles with customers or pretend they were on the phone to get by them. This does not mean they stood there for twenty minutes and sold product. They walked the customer to their destination and then got the expert in that area to assist.

This is not hard to do; you will gain more traction as a manager in customer service if you lead by example and hold your team accountable for a high level of service. Remember, if you demand a high level of service and do not personally follow through it will be noticed by everyone.

The first thing that needs to be spelled out is the organizations expectations of customer service. The management team needs to understand what needs to happen and what will not be tolerated.

Here are some guidelines to get your standards on track:

✓Print the organization's vision statement and customer service policies and understand them.

✓During one of the many managerial meetings held every week, make this one count. You need to discuss why customer service is so important, how does it impact the business and what value it represents to the store. The message has been watered down over the years. You must be specific.

Speak from the heart about your expectations, insincerity aligns with all of the watered down messages. Discuss the vision and policies that relate to the issue. This gives the manager a clear idea of what is expected, what will be tolerated and the consequences of failure. Ask for their commitment to the program.

✓You need to set deadlines for managers to discuss expectations with their teams. The store manager should make an effort to be involved; it shows a commitment to the program. The meetings, regardless if they are in a group or one on one need to convey urgency and importance.

✓If you observe any failures in customer service, it must be addressed immediately with an explanation of what their action represented to the company and what it could have been. This is not an opportunity to embarrass anyone, rather, an educational opportunity. If your organization requires the failure to be documented, do it, this is about consistency.

✓Recognize examples of great service in morning, afternoon or evening store sales-floor meetings. This is a great opportunity to reinforce positive behavior. This should be talked about often. If your company has reporting or rankings in customer service, good or bad, this must be discussed every day without fail.

✓Do not yell, scream or threaten employees or managers to get them customer service centric. A manager's job is to show the value and how this one aspect of daily life fits into the big picture.

If you are not doing well with customer service either through reporting or observation, get the mirror out. Have you set the tone and discussed specific expectations in regards to customer service? If you have not completed some of the steps above, you have work to do before you start pointing the finger at others.

Do not wait until there is a problem to address this

issue. Do not assume if everything seems right that it is. Be proactive and discuss the importance of customer service. You never know when a bad month or customer complaint will work against your efforts.

Kill The Competition

You cannot run the competition out of town. If you are focusing on customer service, it is a great start. Realize that competitor interest in your store varies by location. Some know your store inside and out while others haven't been to see you in a long time. Chances are your focus on the competition is the same, sporadic.

I will be very direct here, if you do not know the advantages your competitor has in your specific market, you are losing sales opportunities. If you have not been inside of your competition in a long time, it speaks volumes about your sales drive and it is not good.

I understand that your organization may have a national view of the competitor and may inform you of their current actions. How does this relate to your local market? Managers need to know the competition and know what to do with that information. It is not enough to know they sell similar things or offer similar services.

The information about competitors must be known at all levels. How well does your store understand the competition? Here is a brief list of items to consider, break out the mirror and answer honestly.

✓ Have you shopped two major competitors in your market in the past 30 days?

✓ During your last competitive visit, did you go with a specific objective in mind or a general visit?

✓ Has your assistant or department level managers been inside the competition in the past 30 days? Did they go with a specific agenda?

✓ What are the similarities in product and services, including customer service initiatives?

✓ Do you know who their top sales people are?

✓ Do you know the advantages they have over your store? Disadvantages?

✓ What was the last plan that you implemented locally to counter act the competition?

✓ When was the last time you discussed a competitor specific issue during a meeting of any kind?

I hope that you were honest when answering these questions. If it was tough to answer some or you could not answer them, you are not alone. Another hopeful thought is that it was unbelievable to you that there were things you did not know. How do you expect to be the best in the market when you do not know your own advantages?

It is unacceptable to be a manager in a store with disregard for the power of competition. I have witnessed many times throughout the years, ignorance in regards to competitors. Ask sales people about a competitor that sits across your parking lot, with cars in front of the building, what customers say about that competitor. I'll get out my crystal ball and come up with the answer, the customer states they do not like the competitor and nobody ever shops there.

This drives me crazy, if nobody shops there, why are they in business? Refuse to accept generalities about competitors. As a manager, you must know the competition intimately and demand that your people know them.

A competitive understanding is required at a deep level. You cannot go into a store, walk the center racetrack and feel you know the competitor. You must go with a specific measure in mind. The objective is to learn something about their business.

Competitor visits should be required for all levels necessary. Store managers, assistants and department managers are a must while others such as big-ticket sales people would benefit from visits as well. They must be structured with a specific purpose. This could be a specific product line or service or program. Ask yourself what you want to learn, what information you want to bring back.

Narrowing down your research of the competitor will ensure focus and value are represented in the visit. Consider the competitive advantages of your research. Do not go with assumptions. If you assume your store does a better job it may skew your research or findings. Go with an open mind set for discovery. If the competition has the advantage it gives you an opportunity to figure out how to counteract it.

After you have visited and researched the competitor there is still more to do. Often a competitive shop is done and the information never really gets utilized. If you have the information, use it to educate your staff. The goal is that no potential customer leaves the store to shop the competition; you already have their pricing and information on their assortment from the competitive shop. This can be especially useful with seasonal items.

Every retailer has a price matching policy; if you want to be competitive, do not be afraid to use it. This is where knowing the competition will help to keep a customer in your building. Get serious about being the final destination for the customer.

You need to develop and mold a competitive program to your store. Where will you receive the most benefit? This is another piece to the puzzle of developing your people and environment. If you are working on morale, developing your team and holding them accountable, leading by example with customer service and taking your competition seriously, you are on your way to improving the viability of your store.

Chapter Seven
Challenging Meetings

Have you ever witnessed a manager or employee meeting where every one left the room energized with a stronger commitment? Me neither. Meetings are typically a long, tired, one-way conversation. The senior manager typically goes on and on about past performance and the current state of sales with no indicator or hint of how to reach the weekly goals.

We sometimes forget what meetings are designed to do. They are necessary to communicate a message and unify the team to work towards one cause, the organization's vision. Most retailers have weekly meetings for managers and department managers; some have meetings for select members of the sales team. Most meetings fail to do much of anything but tell a group of people to work harder while failing to recognize good performances.

Dust Off Your Meetings

It is time to assess the status of your meeting format. If you want a good indicator of the level of motivation your meetings represent, there is an easy observation to make. When the meeting is over, watch the actions of your team as they leave the room. If they are full of energy and discussing what they need to conquer next, your meetings may already be a success. If they are tired, stretching and yawning as they leave the room, you have some work to do.

If your meeting spends a lot of time on the past such as sales last week or month, it really should not. The problem with this, it should be done in a reflective tone but it typically is done as a review or recap. Investing time in recaps for the sake of reading the numbers does not offer learning of any kind.

If your meeting does not encourage participation, people will tune out. If your requirement to attend a meeting is to sit and listen while you talk at the team, there is minimal value. People want to be heard, they want to express opinions and ideas, and they want to contribute to the success of the store. Even an individual that is quiet and does not speak up much has something to say, they just want to be asked.

If your meeting consists of you always having the best solution, people will tune out. I know you may have the most experience in the room, so what! This does not mean your solution is the best possible solution that exists, you have to be willing to listen and credit your team members with the view they bring to the table. This also promotes buy-in, loyalty and commitment. If you are willing to give up those three things because of your ego, you are tearing down morale.

Instead of always having the answer, help your team develop the answer as a collaborative unit. You can be the guide that brings everything together. Remember what I said earlier; surround yourself with people that are smarter than you are in various areas. If you have done this, you will want to hear what they have to say. If you continue to want to be the smartest manager on the block, you will work twice as hard.

If your meetings last for hours and hours, you are wasting valuable, productive time. The goal should be getting everyone out of the room and back to work, not breaking records for how long you can pontificate. You would not tolerate employees in the break room discussing business for hours, right? It is not productive and does not contribute to achieving the vision. Please put everyone out of their misery, prepare and make the content fit a short meeting time frame. This will keep you on topic and from beating a topic to death.

This may all sound a bit negative but it is based in

reality. No one on your staff is going to tell you that they can't stand your meetings and if they enjoy sitting for hours away from the sales floor, that is another problem entirely. The next segment will discuss creating a new agenda to keep the content tight and the meeting moving.

A New Agenda - Managers

Out with the old and in with the new. You have made many strides to improve and create a learning environment. The next step is to turn the unproductive weekly meetings into a productive, concise learning opportunity. I am not opposed to meetings. They are a necessity. In fact, I suggest adding a meeting to the daily managerial routine as a way to combine efforts.

The following is a list of suggestions for senior management meetings. Consider what will work in your store and be open to change.

✓Meetings that exceed 2 hours are unproductive, try to fit the content into 1 hour for maximum productivity.

✓Create an agenda for the meeting. This is nothing fancy, an outline to be used to keep the meeting on track. Note the topic and the amount of time you wish to give it. The hardest part is sticking to it. Keep the meeting on track, straying from the time allotted typically means you are going into overkill with the topic.

✓Send a short email out a few days before the meeting with an outline and ask the team to be prepared to discuss the topics. This will stimulate thinking prior to the meeting and encourage participation. This will also help to move along through the topic as the team had time to think about it as opposed to processing the information on the spot.

✓Allow time for participation from the team. This is necessary to promote inclusion, gain insight from diverse perspective and strengthen the commitment to a topic. The trick here is keeping your staff on topic and realistic. They cannot drift into wonderland with dreams of changing entire systems or million-dollar technology fixes that are not probable at a local level.

If you keep the meeting moving forward every week and cover topics in a clear, concise manner, your staff will learn to do the same. At first, you can mention the time assigned to each topic to ensure the remaining time spent is quick and to the point.

✓Ensure your management meeting reviews opportunities within the store. This could be with product lines, services or customer service. Whatever the issue is you need to get input and make a decision as a group of how to remedy the situation. If there is a policy in place, how will your team adhere, implement or remain compliant.

Utilize reports to identify future opportunities. Do not dwell on past performances unless you connect them to future opportunities. How can we improve this performance? Do not rattle off a continuous line of numbers, they are over and done. Instead, focus on one or two areas and discuss solutions to repair or build upon successes.

This is part of the education process. Part of developing your team is helping them with identifying opportunities within the store and creating solutions. If you sent the agenda out as discussed earlier, your team will be prepared to discuss the topics.

Another tactic here to develop your team is to assign 1 to 2 members a different topic to cover during the meeting. Ask them to discuss a problem or opportunity and present possible realistic solutions. The solutions must be possible within the current resources and not outlandish requests. Take this opportunity to teach them how to reflect on the problem and constructively critique their solutions. Ask for input from the team. If the solution needs further time, assign additional research and deadlines. Once a decision is reached by the team and approved by you, the plan needs your support.

✓Discuss the competition. Chapter six outlined

competitive practices to coach, train and develop your team. Discussing their findings is vital to utilizing the knowledge to improve your competitive edge. This is another opportunity to assign a staff member to speak briefly about a competitive issue and present solutions.

✓After the major issues have been discussed, every meeting should end asking for a commitment from each manager. The commitment should include continuing to work towards the organization's vision and an understanding of what it means to the store in terms of morale and success. If this becomes a soapbox moment for you, learn to keep it brief. Nothing kills sincerity more than listening to the same speech every week. Keep it simple and brief.

The goal of this structure is to keep the meeting flowing to remain interesting and educational. There will be times that you have to take the team to task on an issue, keep it brief, state your expectations and offer any solutions. Then move on to the next topic. Think about the amount of payroll you have in one room, they should come out of the meeting with something that helps them to develop. Developing your managers means that you are improving the potential success of your business.

A New Agenda - Department Managers

The department manager meetings are conducted by assistant store managers in retailers. There are retailers that require the store manager to preside over the meeting. The structure is similar to the senior manager meeting. There must be a higher level of learning in these meetings. These managers are the future senior leaders of the organization.

✓Meetings should last approx. ½ hour to 1 hour. Make the content fit this timeframe.

✓Create an agenda for the meeting. This meeting will typically focus on task/ product opportunities. Do not forget development opportunities for the manager. This includes how to develop their people.

✓Send a short email out a few days before the meeting with an outline and ask the team to be prepared to discuss the topics. This will continue the development cycle. Department managers are often not asked for their input, yet they are the closest layer of management to the employees and customers.

✓Allow time for participation from the team. This is vital for department managers to grow in their position. Listen to their ideas and suggestions. Anything that can be logically and reasonably implemented will provide a great example for future participation and will further buy-in.

✓Ensure your management meeting reviews opportunities within the store. This could be with product lines, services or customer service. This step is the same for senior managers, it is that important. You will learn a great deal from department level managers in regards to opportunities. They are closer to pulse of the consumer. Leave your ego at the door and listen to them.

This area is the same as for senior managers and is simply restated. Identify focus opportunities and assign 1 to 2 members a different topic to cover during the meeting. Ask them to discuss a problem or opportunity and present possible realistic solutions. The solutions must be possible within the current resources and not outlandish requests.

Take this opportunity to teach them how to reflect on the problem and constructively analyze their solutions. Ask for input from the team. If the solution needs further time, assign additional research and deadlines. They will need additional guidance that will benefit from an experienced point of view. Once a decision is reached by the team and approved by you, the plan needs your support.

✓Discuss the competition. Department managers should be assigned to complete competitive shops. The shops should be focused on a product or service in their area of responsibility. The findings should be discussed along with potential solutions. Reminder, keep the meeting on track. Department managers are viewing the business from a more detailed point of view and they tend to want to review every small issue, which may seem major but have many other priorities ahead of it. Your job is to help them define priorities according to impact on the business.

✓This step is the same as senior manager meetings. After the major issues have been discussed, every meeting should end asking for a commitment from each department manager. The commitment should include continuing to work towards the organization's vision and defining what it means to the store in terms of morale and success.

A New Agenda – Sales People

This is another kind of meeting all together and typically exists for big-ticket sales people. This is another example of misguided content in its current form that wastes time and costs the store money. If your meetings are productive and your people learn something of value during the meeting, you are in the minority.

There is a better way to handle these meetings to ensure your team progresses and selling skills are sharpened. If you shy away from coaching, training and developing employees in a particular department due to your lack of product knowledge, think differently. A manager's role should focus on customer service, closing sales and selling skills. At times, product categories are irrelevant.

Your sales team should have resources to learn more about product but they have no one to help them close sales. If you have team members that are currently failing in a sales capacity, get out the mirror for the next test. If you have invested selling skills training into the individual, it may be time to follow policy to part ways. If you have not done anything besides tell your team to hit their numbers, who is at fault?

The following is a list of content for meetings to consider. Use a meeting as an opportunity to advance your teams skills. This list is viable regardless of the facilitator; often an assistant manager leads these meetings.

✓The meeting should be held weekly and last no longer than 1 hour.

✓The manager should have a meeting agenda to keep the meeting moving forward. This will also keep the meeting on time and on topic.

✓The agenda should be emailed or hand distributed to allow the employees to begin applying thought to the various topics. This will grant time for employee preparation to ensure the meeting does not get bogged down with unnecessary discovery questions.

✓Something to consider with employee preparation is having them bring any open leads or quotes to discuss. You do not have to review each one, shuffle them, pull out 2-3 and discuss the status of the quote. This should be done in a learning capacity, not with the intention of embarrassment.

The review should consist of challenging questions such as:

- What do we know about the customer?
- Why haven't they purchased the items?
- Who is our competition for the quote?
- When was the last time the employee spoke directly to the customer?
- Did the employee ask for the sale? Did they ask the customer directly why they have not purchased yet?
- Do they understand the variables, such as time frame, quantity, available credit, competitive pricing, etc?

The design of the questions should stimulate thought around ways the sale could have been closed. This offers the group an opportunity to discuss ways to close the sale and learn as a team. The expectation should be clear that you would do this every week to help develop forward thinking skills. If you are relying on your team to automatically know the customer at a deep level, you need to look back at the segments on development and accountability.

✓When reviewing sales numbers, be brief. The past is over and done, leverage the past results to uncover future opportunities. Frame this area of the meeting as what have we learned and how can we sustain success or develop an opportunity.

✓Your sales team should be scheduled individually to shop the competition. The destination should be specific to a product or service to provide usable information. Do not send them to the competition to just look around. Nothing gets accomplished here.

The results should be discussed during the meeting with the employee offering solutions to overcome any disadvantages. This is your opportunity to place their thoughts in reality. Help them develop viable solutions to combat the competitor, they are learning how to overcome objections when they are doing this, and you are creating buy-in.

✓Ask for continued commitment to the organization's vision.

Make the meeting more than just numbers with the threat of immediate improvement, this teaches nothing. Make the time invested count and the team will continue to improve. Change the direction of your meeting to align with productive goals and learning.

A New Agenda - Morning, Afternoon, Evening Sales Floor Meetings

These are daily meetings that most retailers require, sometimes-called huddles. They gather employees working at that time together to discuss various topics. These usually occur right on the sales floor in an attempt to make it a quick hit. These meetings are somewhat effective; if there is a mass message or change, it gets to more people.

The meeting's tone varies by the manager that presides over them. Some are serious, cover a bunch of numbers, and speak about immediate improvements based on reporting. While others lead the meeting through light conversation while adding an occasional win or something to note. They are usually pleasant but uninformative.

These meetings are golden opportunities to reinforce good behavior and give real life examples. These meetings should be quick, no more than 15 minutes. If you are prepared for the meeting that should be all the time you need. This does not require much preparation; you want a rough outline to stay on topic and within the allotted time.

Performance issues should be discussed often. Total sales should be mentioned quickly unless you have a future learning opportunity to attach to it. The basis of the meeting should be around recognition of performances, which provide a great way for employees to learn.

You can recognize Mary for her credit performance

yesterday and ask her to say a few words about her performance. You can make a big deal out of a first time event for an employee, maybe their big project sold. Talk about what it takes to have exceptional performance. It does not always have to be a measurable item, recognition for great customer service through observation or customer feedback are solid examples.

You can discuss change or negative performances through a learning lens. Do not get angry and display your temper on the sales floor. It is unprofessional but more importantly it does not teach anything at all. Telling someone to get something right will not suffice; you would not have the issue if they could get it right.

Clearly define the process, there is not a problem stating your disappointments but think about how you are sending people back to work. If you tear them down, you have drained the momentum right out of the building.

I'm not saying they should never hear the bad stuff, they definitely should. It should be in the context of how to improve and what you expect versus telling them to get better or they are fired. Tell them what the behavior or ranking is and get them back on track through expectations in alignment with the organizations vision.

Every meeting should include customer service, if there is reporting it should be discussed. Positive experiences should be presented to the group; negative individual experiences should be handled one on one with the employee and not made an example of in front of the group. You want the meeting to provide energy and motivation to encourage employees to perform at a high level.

Another great area to discuss is any incentive programs or contests for employees that are currently running. If there is an opportunity to earn money for things such as customer service scores or credit accounts, discuss it at every meeting. The brief discussion should include where you are and where you need to be to for employees to maximize the reward.

A New Agenda - Managerial One A Day

I know what you are thinking, not another meeting. If you have evaluated your current meeting structure, you have probably found some time to shave off of the meetings. I am not looking to spend that time for you but there is another meeting that works well for the management staff.

The typical retail schedule requires opening managers and closing managers. There are typically processes that need to be completed between the two shifts. A quick update meeting that brings the senior managers together for 10 minutes ensures all processes are accounted for. This should be between the two shifts at a time before the dinner break of the evening managers.

This gives the manager's time to review what was accomplished and what still needs to be done. This includes customer issues, employee issues, special projects and current news. This should be informal and quick. You will find communication vastly improved and better employee direction through an understanding of what needs to be accomplished.

No long agenda here, try this and see if you notice an improvement in the managerial team environment. You may also notice an improvement in daily tasks and this is especially helpful in a broken building, as we will discuss in a later chapter.

Chapter Eight

Credit & Miscellaneous Income

This chapter may not apply to everyone. Most retailers openly solicit credit. This is either their house brand of credit or established forms of credit. The same goes for extended warranties or protection warranties sold on merchandise. This category has exploded in stores as retail giants realize the tremendous profits and consumer loyalty these programs inspire.

Along with the realized profits, these programs drive realized pressure for the managers and the sales floor employees. The problem with training employees to solicit these programs is assigning goals without educating the employee on the value they represent. The employee is left to ask each customer in a half embarrassed tone if the customer wants these things. It is no surprise that opportunity remains to capture sales through these vehicles. We will discuss each one separately.

I Get No Credit

There are a few types of employees when it comes to credit acquisition. The one's that go after it and are always at the top of the heap, those who never try to get an application and those that give a marginal effort and stumble into a few. This variation takes on a life of its own as managers come to expect a particular performance from an individual, if they know at all.

If you are unaware of the individual credit performances of your team, you are to blame for missed opportunities. Store managers have to rely on their assistants to know the individual performances. Credit acquisition, depending on your organization's policies, should be on the plate of all of the employees. Think about your organization's vision statement, does credit acquisition align with the desire to offer great service?

Credit can contribute to a higher level of customer service. Too often the employee or manager puts themselves in the shoes of the customer and may not solicit credit because they believe it is detrimental. You will hear employees tell stories about high interest rates and how they cannot contribute to consumer debt. I will tell you, they are in the wrong job.

Employees that have a moral issue with offering credit do not belong on the sales floor, the same goes for extended warranties. Credit is not a religion, no one is asking them to convert. Let the customer decide what is right for them. I personally do not want a retail employee making a decision for my credit health. It is none of their business.

What does your company require? If it is a requirement that employees offer credit during every transaction, they should be. If a manager is not supporting the initiative, are they the right person for the job? If the manager does not see the big picture, their vision is influenced by personal believes and at the end of the day who asked for their opinion on a policy?

I am sure some would consider my words strong in this area. Can you see how credit plays an important role for driving sales in the whole organization? We will discuss more about recognizing the contribution of individual components to the whole in chapter 10.

I have heard every excuse for failure in this area and managers experience some discomfort in holding employees accountable. Most base it on personal experiences of going into a retailer and being hounded for credit. I totally get it, at times, it can be irritating but credit is a necessity to capture more of the wallet share today.

There are many credit offers in stores today for the consumer. The responsibility level of the consumer to handle credit is not your concern. Your competitor is soliciting credit. If you think a customer is considering the irritation of credit solicitation upon which retailer they will visit, I disagree. In fact, I think it may just be the opposite especially in the case of in-house brand credit cards. The customer may decide to buy from your store because they have or can get credit.

Credit is now a part of the competitive advantage for retailers. Managers need to help employees identify with the value of credit to a customer and the organization. This can also be an exercise on a competitive visit for a manager or employee, as well.

You need to review your performance, the policy, the expectation of your boss and get serious. Next, you will need to consider the following to get your program in gear.

✓The first step is to understand your credit products and the value in each.

✓ You need to create credit goals for different areas of the store. Base this on your budget, past performance and potential. They must be realistic.

✓If your organization has training available, get everyone trained, especially if your store is not performing well in credit.

✓Leverage the reporting and store comparisons during manager meetings. They need to understand the expectations going forward. If you have any supporting company details to add or that assist with educating on the value of credit, use them. Everyone sees value differently, schedule time for a discussion and most importantly discuss credit goals. Make sure you get their commitment to improve.

✓Repeat the above step for the department manager meeting and sales team meetings. Place emphasis on showing them the value of credit. A good example is utilizing it as a tool to close a sale. Any real life examples to support the positive influence of credit would be appropriate here. End the meeting with their commitment to solicit credit.

✓Discuss credit performance at every morning, afternoon, evening huddles on the sales floor. Recognize great performances and new contributors. Ensure you briefly discuss value, any real-life current stories and reporting that contributes to understanding value. Discuss ways to overcome objections. Lastly, discuss the store goal in relation to the current performance. Finish the meeting with gaining their commitment and buy-in.

A real life example for me occurred in a big box retailer. I never really paid much attention to credit performance, our store was middle of the pack and there were greater concerns. Until our mediocre performance embarrassed me on a conference call with my boss, now you have my attention.

I started taking a hard look at employee contributions and attitudes towards credit. I noticed that employees were not very comfortable with soliciting credit, which means they did not understand the value. There were a few bright performers that consistently opened new accounts, mainly to enable them to close sales on big-ticket products. There were also employees that had not opened an account in years; the environment created an "I don't care" attitude. Managers, including myself, solidified this attitude through no coaching and no accountability.

I followed the plan listed above and started to relate the value of credit to all layers of management and employees. I got the pushback mentioned earlier of not pressuring customers like the competitor and pushback on established goals.

I discussed the performance and goals at the morning sales floor meetings. This is where I recognized great performances and new comers to opening accounts. I constantly discussed the value to our store. A report that was particularly helpful to relay this message was one that showed the opened accounts over the past selected amount of days and the open to buy amount that it represented to our company. This really reached the individuals who had no idea what credit meant to the store.

I initially offered the group a real example of opening 8 in-house accounts over the weekend and asked them how much they think it represented in customer open to buy. They all guessed different amounts such as $20k, $30k and lower. The actual amount for the example was $80k on those accounts. They started to get the importance. I knew they were on board when they would call me for an account they opened and talked in terms of open to buy. It took awhile and constant reinforcement but we raised the bar and expectation in credit for the district.

✓Discuss the offerings from competitors. Use competitive information to compare and offer ways to overcome objections with customers.

✓Address poor performers through coaching and additional training, assign them a partner and get your department manager involved. They should not be ignored, remember everyone sees value differently; they just do not see it yet. Make them accountable but give them help as well.

You must understand the credit contribution to your store and the organization before you begin coaching, training and developing employees. Learn the benefits of each offering and be versed in the competitive advantage.

Miscellaneous Income

Retailers offer different types and variations of replacement warranties, product extended warranties and preventative maintenance agreements. These warranties have fallen victim to a bad rap over the last ten years. The word on the street is that they are a big money grab for the retailer for something that many people never use.

These warranties reflect an individual's risk taking nature. I'm sure you have been faced with the decision, do I take a chance that nothing will go wrong or should I protect my purchase? People are all over the board on this topic. Some people see them as a rip-off and never buy them while others like the peace of mind perspective.

Regardless of a customer's position on warranties, it is the employee's job to represent it well. This goes hand in hand with credit, your employee's attitude towards these warranties impact their ability to present them.

If your store does not perform well, get out the mirror. This time think about your attitude toward warranties and how you represent the value to employees, than look at your level of interaction with the team. If you are negative or never discuss this area, they will rarely be successful.

You can just hear the religious connotations creeping in when a manager or employee states they do not believe in them. In the next breath, they discuss that they are nothing but a moneymaker for the organization. Last time I checked retailers were in business to make money, it does nice things like adds payroll to the store. When I hear excuses, it equates to a complete lack of understanding of the value that warranties represent.

Another great observation is that products should last longer than the warranty or it is junk. Does anyone still believe products are made, as they were 50 years ago, to last forever? If you believe products should still be made this way, get your head out of the past. If products were made the old-fashioned way, you would not want to pay for how much they would cost.

Products are more sophisticated today, they are made to accomplish different things and the economics to design a product is a competitive situation. For example, would you buy a washing machine today that was made to last twice as long for three times the price of a competitor that is selling a standard version? You might but most people will not.

Stop making excuses for not learning what the warranty does and the benefits to consumers. Not to be rude, once again no one asked you for your input on selling these warranties. If you can sell products through a feature to benefit structure, you can honestly represent the value of extended warranties or service policies.

Stop making decisions for me; much like credit I can make up my own mind on what represents value in my life. I personally buy many of these warranties, not out of obligation or to prove a point. Simply because I am not handy, cannot fix things and I really do not want to use my time that way. I do not buy them all but I feel comfortable that I am protected for a period of time.

It is difficult to pin down a one-size fits all approach to improving in this area. Let's discuss some of the broader points that should be considered in your store planning.

✓You need to compare your store performance to your sister stores and to the organization's budget.

✓Review the individual performance of your team in comparison to goals.

✓You need to have a deep understanding of the warranty programs offered. You also need to know what your competition offers as well.

✓If your organization has a training program on warranties, get your HR manager to schedule each employee to complete the training as a starting point or reintroduction.

✓Set goals for each employee group on the sales floor.

✓Discuss reporting and current performance during senior management meetings. Discuss the value of the warranty programs and what they represent to customers, the store as well as the organization. Ensure you clearly define expectations, goals and gain their commitment.

✓Discuss the value of warranty programs at the department manager meeting. This will take more time, expect objections and push back. They have probably received push back from the sales teams who "do not believe" in warranties. Plan to discuss overcoming objections and gain their commitment to the organizations vision and this program.

✓Discuss or reintroduce your expectations of this program during sales floor weekly meetings. You will receive considerable objections to the program. You will need to represent value to the customer, the store and the organization. You must clearly define the expectations. They must understand their accountability and consequences of their performance. Do not dwell on the negatives, instead suggest that further training may be required if results are not achieved. Follow company policy on performance to address future substandard performance.

✓Discuss results during morning, afternoon, evening sales floor huddles. Recognize great performances; ask employees to share success stories. Briefly discuss the value of the program and the benefits to customers. Discuss store performance in relation to the goal and the organization's vision.

✓Do not forget to discuss the offerings from competitors during the meetings. This does not have to be discussed during every meeting, add it occasionally to keep the team up to date. Do not hesitate to add warranty programs to the competitive shops that you schedule as a learning tool.

✓Address poor performers through additional coaching and training. Schedule them with another employee that excels in this area. Be sure to follow your company's policies on performance to be consistent with all employees. Be sure they understand the program and consequences of future performance.

Chapter Nine
The Broken Building

There is a pretty good chance, if you have a long retail career that you may be assigned to a store that has numerous problems. You may accept the challenge willingly or by force, either way you are facing a monumental task of "fixing" everything that is broken.

There is no single path to success in this situation. It will call upon every organization and prioritization skill that you have. There are usually two elements at work that are causing a majority of the problems, morale and accountability. If you go in looking to "clean house" and start from scratch you shift the environment from lazy to hostile.

The fact is that you are stuck with the resources for the immediate future. How do you know if the management team or employees or both require some degree of replacement or if they have never been coached, trained or developed? You need to make an assessment to determine what you need. Making rushed decisions may not produce the desired result you are seeking. Remember, this process will take time; it is not an overnight fix.

What Have I Gotten Myself Into?

You will be asking yourself this question not long after you are immersed in a broken environment. It will seem overwhelming at first until you are organized. Being organized requires a plan. You will not survive long if you do not have a plan to follow regardless of your experience or skill set.

Planning is tough because issues are not flush on the surface; there are some you will come across that you never expected. How do you plan for the unknown? This can be answered by understanding there will be the unknown, expect it. You will come across many obstacles, stay organized and do not get rattled.

You need to think of the rebuilding process in three categories: people, processes and presentation. These are three separate aspects, considering them individually will allow three things to be happening simultaneously. The people element is much more complex and requires a longer period of time to evolve. Presentation is typically the quickest and easiest impact to make. Processes will typically require getting organized.

Presentation

We will start here because it is the easiest impact to make. If you have been with the company for a period of time you probably have a pretty good handle on how the store should look. If you are unsure, you will likely know where to find the plans or your staff will point you in the right direction.

If you are new to the organization, the best thing you can do, if possible, is travel to another store and look at the visual standards. You will need to ask questions about where to find merchandise plans and review what is required with your supervisor. You will need to get the team together, either way, to begin getting the building back to standards.

The following is a list for a store manager to consider for the initial meeting.

✓You need to walk through the store and take general notes about each area. Nothing elaborate here and it is not meant to take hours. This gives you points of reference to discuss.

✓This meeting should have the senior staff and department managers. This is a great opportunity to get the message out and get clean up in motion. If you only direct it towards the senior staff, it may delay getting the process started when you include the time for the staff to repeat your words to department heads.

Let's be honest, if the department managers were held accountable by the senior staff, the store would not be visually broken. The senior staff let it happen. They suffered no recourse. This is not an opportunity for you to tell the staff your personal feelings on their performance, even though you may want to express your thoughts loudly.

It is a time to discuss the need for change. You need to motivate them to change. Tell them where the current standards of the building are, typically ranking reports help to clarify the picture, and where you will be through a team effort. Be clear that change begins right now.

✓If there is a company program in place that reviews the condition of departments within the store, use it and stick to it. If there is not a current program, for the sake of organization and recovery, create one. This will allow further monitoring of conditions while you continue to work through the rest of the mess.

An example of a store conditions program may be a weekly walk sheet that senior leaders develop with the department managers to create a list of presentation standards that need to be addressed. This does a few things, it forces collaboration between senior staff members and their department managers. Next, it creates a chain of accountability. If the standards do not improve, where does the problem exist? Ensure a deadline is set for the first time the process is used and on a continual basis.

This process should be quick with a manageable workload for the department team. If the workload is extreme the staff member has to pull resources to get the job done and pitch in themselves at times. You are holding the senior staff member accountable while they are addressing their department head. This creates a learning, growing and developing mentality.

The department manager should take the weekly walk sheet and create individual lists for their team. You are now creating an accountability piece to help the department manager as well. This may sound like a lot of paperwork but the store is broken and you need to coach, train and develop your team to make better decisions. Communicate a deadline for the process, initially and on a weekly basis.

✓You must state the expectations very clearly. Tie everything into the organization's vision. How can you give great service if the building is a mess and shelves are not full? They need to understand the value and the cost associated with a broken environment.

✓Do not start anything new if you do not plan to hold your people accountable and you do not plan to review consistently. Beware; if you start a bunch of new processes and rules and follow up on none of them, you are doing more damage than good. The staff will not take anything with a sense of urgency, why should they, your lack of follow up is proof the plans are not important.

✓Discuss presentation standards at every meeting until they are where you need them to be. Point out great improvements. This is where having the managerial one a day meetings in the late afternoon will allow you to be briefed on everything that needs to be accomplished.

✓Ask the team for their commitment to a new, improved store.

People

This is the most complex yet rewarding area of rebuilding the environment. This will also take the most time to change. Your team, both managers and employees, are unsure of what to expect of you. In a broken building morale is typically low, trust in managers is non-existent and most feel they do not have worth to the organization. There are a lot of feelings and emotions happening at one time.

You have to expect that people will be reserved at first until they see what direction you will settle into. The long-term employees have seen it all, the good managers and the bad. The question in their minds is which side of the spectrum you are on. You need to earn respect and trust. You cannot demand it.

Your people understand the difference between a manager that really cares about them and the business and those who are not on the same team. You need to begin the new team environment by spending a lot of time on the sales floor initially to understand the current state. Here are some things to consider when it comes to the people element.

✓The first and best thing to do is be visible. Be on the sales floor and lead by example, talk with employees and customers. This allows you to gain insight into issues that exist and connect with people. Chances are the last manager was never seen, only heard when there was a problem. This does not mean you should be involved with detailed tasks that will take you away from the big picture. Straighten shelves as you walk, help open boxes as you talk, be helpful and prepared to move on, as well.

✓Next, be present at morning, afternoon, evening huddles

and if your company does not require at least one a day, consider it. This is your opportunity to get the team motivated. Do not stand there and complain about the stores' current state. Instead, discuss the organization's vision and what is needed to do to get there. Do this in small pieces, too much information overwhelms people and they give up before they start.

Utilize reporting to discuss great performances, do not focus on one area of the store, and try to include different areas during the meetings in a given week. Discuss opportunity areas, the current state and desired state to reach goals. Tell them how to get there, give them examples of real life scenarios. Highlight an individual's performance and have them speak about it.

You need to be energetic, upbeat, and motivational and leave the team with a feeling of it can be done. The meetings should be quick, refer to Chapter Seven for further details on meetings. Items to consider including any contests currently running, customer service scores or observations and credit/ warranty performance.

✓You should attend sales team meetings. If your company does not require these types of meetings, consider them. This quick once a week meeting will help sharpen the selling skills of your team. It should be led by a senior manager in the store. You do not need to be there for the entire meeting, pop in and discuss the wins and where improvement is still needed.

✓Coach, train, develop your managers as we have discussed in chapter four. The first half of this book can be used as a guide for a broken building. You need to focus on employee morale, development and accountability.

✓Working with the HR manager, ensure all required training is current and consider additional training when possible such as credit, warranties and customer service training.

✓Read Chapters 2, 3 and 4, they focus on strengthening the people element in your store.

Processes

This part of the repair or rebuild usually follows policies and procedures. There is typically not a lot of room for creativity here and that is a good thing, you have enough to do without creating new processes. You need to focus on compliancy and getting your team back on track.

The first step is determining what needs to be accomplished daily. Your organization may have a list of what needs to be addressed and the timeframes. This would make life a lot easier here. Follow the list and define your expectations and consequences to your management staff if requirements are not met. This area is all about accountability.

If you do not have a set list, you need to create one for daily use. I know it may seem there is a tremendous amount to do between check sheets and meetings but you need to leverage ways of organizing a large body of people. You need to unify the team towards the vision.

The check sheet should have two sections, one should be dedicated to daily processes and the other should reflect what is due for the week. There are many things to review daily for management that it becomes difficult at times to ensure something does not fall between the cracks.

This check sheet should be initiated by the opening manager. The sheet should be simple with the name of the action or report or system to review or complete with a line for the manager to initial. There may be some actions that need to be reviewed multiple times per day such as a customer complaint screen or delivery notifications. The name of the action can simply have a few short lines for the am/pm managers to initial.

The form should not be cluttered, no philosophies or threats, simply state the action that is required with the line next to it. The top of the form should have a title with a line for the date. The operations or administrative manager should have a file folder to place completed copies, keep for a month and then discard. This should not add time or task to managers, it is only a way to keep organized.

The beauty of this simple sheet is that it can be reviewed at the managers one a day meeting. This is a great way to start the meeting and gives the team an overview of what needs to be accomplished for the remainder of the day. This checklist will ensure that nothing is missed or overlooked or not assigned.

The list is a win for a store manager. It ensures critical elements are taken care of everyday and completed while you are not at the store, as well. You will also be enforcing accountability via the initials on the check sheet. The team will have an understanding of what needs to be completed. If something is missed, you can address individually.

The value of this sheet should be obvious but do not assume everyone understands or gets the connection. Tie the need to ensure compliancy to the big picture. Every action should be aligned with the organization's vision. The question you need to answer for the team is how does ensuring processes are complete contribute to the success of the store and company?

Turn This Ship Around

Among the least motivating things a manager can say, "Turn this ship around" is the worst. If you have never heard this, let me explain. This is the go to line for managers that are frustrated with a certain aspect of their business. This is also a very tempting trap for a store manager in a broken building to fall into.

Instead of taking the time to discover the root cause of a problem or issue, they assemble the responsible parties and issue their sound words of advice "Get this ship turned around." If you are guilty of using this approach, or something like it, I hope it made you feel like you solved a problem but in reality, nothing was accomplished.

This type of approach is generally used as a threat or assertion of power. Basically, it is saying I'm telling you to make this situation better without offering my advice, opinion, collaboration or support. The manager or employee is left with the message of just do it. The store manager leaves this conversation feeling they have made a contribution.

Let's talk about the reality of this situation. If a manager or employee knew how to improve the business or understood the problem, they would have probably done that already. A discussion about the problem and help with planning would go a lot further. You do not have to help construct the plan. Have the team create a plan for improvement for your review. This offers your guidance and buy-in of the final plan.

The collaboration with the planning stage lets the team know that you are in this to help. You are recognizing the contribution of the team's solution to the problem and linking it to your responsibility, which is the whole store or the big picture. The problem with demanding something be fixed is the isolation of the problem as a singular event. In other words, you are not considering the impact of a small part of the store on the rest of the store.

The Big Picture

The big picture is the ability of a manager to look beyond one corner of the store. This vision can include the store or entire organization. Typically, a manager will only consider the impact of a problem or solution on a department or people that are directly impacted. This is a narrow view approach in management and does not encourage individual or team growth.

In a retail store, there is often a focus on fixing an immediate problem without giving much thought to the further implications of the solution. In a broken building, to focus on one element would create a temporary fix without a lasting effect.

The store is really comprised of many different mechanisms that work together to function as a whole. A mechanism can be a department, product line, staffing, policies, merchandising, advertising, training, inventory, etc.

When you create change for one mechanism, you are ultimately affecting others. For example, if you are reviewing departments and recognize the need for additional staffing in an area, you must consider where a position will be cut. When you cut that position, to be payroll compliant, what impact will it have on customers, surrounding departments, current staff hours, ability to complete tasks, presentation, miscellaneous income, etc?

The worst thing to do in a broken building assignment is make decisions without thinking them through. Making uneducated decisions will create new problems, especially in unfamiliar terrain. This is not to say decisions require weeks of thought, you need to react to your environment, but you need to take educated risks. There is nothing wrong with gambling on a new change that you have initiated to work, just make educated changes.

Making educated changes, that will last, requires an understanding of how that solution will affect all of the components they may touch. You need to use forward thinking to reduce or eliminate barriers. Put your solution on paper in a hand drawn box and then connect that box to every possible area that may be affected. Learn to look at the whole system and how it is affected.

Do the same solution exercise with your staff when they have to create solutions to fix problems. When you do this, you are making the decision process clearer for you and for them. The best part, you are developing their skills to see beyond their own corner of the store. This is a necessary trait to move from a manager to leader.

Chapter Ten

Managers as Leaders

I'm not sure if you noticed but I did not use the term leader very often throughout this book. This was by design. The term is so loosely thrown around these days it has adapted to any meaning that an individual may want it to. The word is so overused that its impact has been diminished. If you don't believe me, research books on the topic and you may go blind scrolling through the hundreds of available titles.

Leadership may have varied meanings but there are areas that most can agree. Leadership is a transition from management. It is a role that calls upon developed expertise as a foundation to enable forward thinking. A manager executes and a leader is the visionary thinker, both are critical roles. Whatever your specific definition, which one are you?

Which are you allowed to be? The questions should be answered separately and honestly.

Let Me Be a Leader

Does this sound familiar? The retail environment has not evolved much from command and control. The fact that you may be a leader does not necessarily mean that you will be allowed to be one. Before we get into stifled leadership, you need to determine where your skill set currently resides.

Store managers typically tout themselves as leaders but in some cases they are misleading themselves. You may be in a leadership role but may still be developing as a leader. There is nothing wrong with development; half of this book is about the topic.

I believe leadership qualities are developed through self-initiative, experience, analytical thought and relationships with people. In a sense, you need to be able to connect with people, show them value in your vision of the future and how to get there. This is not easy for some and will never be obtainable for others. It requires an instilled sense of motivation, a deep understanding of the business and people and managerial maturation.

The problem with the current retail environment is that it does not encourage growth from manager to leader. So many decisions are made from a central home office location that there is nothing left to do but execute at a local level.

The local market focus has been replaced with a "we can't afford for you to get things wrong so here is a basic universal approach" mentality.

As a store manager or senior manager there is not much that can be done with this approach, other than to execute at a high level. I am not saying that the organization is wrong with the approach; there are probably a good percentage of managers in position that may not have the ability or capability to evolve into a leader. The company needs to protect its ability to capitalize on as many dollars as possible.

This may have you shouting, "Let me be a leader" if you walk in leadership shoes. You may have more influence and ability to grow than you think. You need to consider the many variables under your control. You may not be able to determine what goes on an end cap, even though you may know the local market better than someone that is several states away, influencing product may not be within your reach. The more important fact is, people are under your umbrella to coach, train and develop.

Reflections of Leadership

The first transition from retail manager to leader is learning to see the store as a whole. We discussed this in the last chapter, when you consider the positive and negative influences throughout the store and how change aligns with the organization's vision you are beginning to evolve.

For the store "whole" to become natural in your decision-making, it requires the ability to think back as well as forward. Reflection is often ignored and seldom considered important in the course of a day. Reflecting is time dedicated to thinking back through decisions that you have made and evaluating them for potential alternate courses of action.

You need to create time to look back, think of a past or recent situation and how you handled it. What was the result? What were your other considerations to resolve the issue? What would have happened if you used another action? What would have happened if you used a completely different option?

Think through the situation and consider all of the variables that you can now see through hindsight. The art of reflection is considering the outcomes that could have been in comparison to your actual choice to determine what may have worked better. You can think through the situation, apply the outcomes and then go backwards to determine if you had the resources for that particular action to work.

Reflection is a valuable teaching tool, as well. You are reflecting when you discuss a situation with one of your managers and the actions you took, at that time, to resolve an issue or enhance something. Now, take it a step further. What if you discussed the situation and asked your manager what they would have done? What if you asked them to evaluate another course of action that you considered at the time?

These types of discussions stimulate forward thinking. The decisions that your managers will make should be based on past experience, reflection and future outcomes. This is a part of developing your team in a leadership environment.

Developing Leaders

You can help your managers make the transition from managers that simply execute to leaders or higher-level managers that are forward thinkers. If you look through the material presented throughout this book you will find it building towards developing a higher tiered manager or for those with capabilities, a developing leader.

Not everyone will develop into a leader; there are some managers that do not want leadership responsibilities. For those that want to improve in their current role or seek higher aspirations, they must push themselves beyond the limitations of the retail environment. There is no one inside of the retail structure that will guide you through developing stages of leadership. Everyone is pressed for time and your boss just simply wants things done.

You need an assessment of foundational practices to develop leadership. Where are you, honestly, with the following areas?

- Reflection
- Assessing the capabilities of your staff
- Hiring or promoting managers
- Aligning actions of you and your team with the organization's vision
- Holding your staff accountable
- Your staff's ability to hold their people accountable
- Coaching, training and developing your staff
- Your staff's ability to coach, train, develop their teams
- Understanding your competition
- Your staff's understanding of the competition
- Your understanding of the store and organization as a whole
- Your staff's understanding of the store as a whole
- Your team's performance with credit and warranties, etc

This book is not meant to offer a leadership path. There are volumes of books on the subject. This book is meant to help you assess your current capabilities on the road to leadership.

Retail is a tough and challenging business, your job as a manager is not easy but can be rewarding. Consider your path and your aspirations, self-assess to develop in areas that need to be improved. This is not an overnight process in any aspect; it takes a considerable period of time. I wish you all of the success you desire and are willing to work for.

ABOUT THE AUTHOR

Richard Bell has been in retail management for the past 22 years. He has held various positions in small and big-box retailers from department manager to store, district and regional leadership. He has a Master of Science in Management with a specialization in Change Leadership. Richard is also a Certified Business Coaching Specialist and Certified Business Consultant with a green belt certification in Six Sigma, as well. He resides in Pittsburgh, PA with his wife and two children.

BusinessManagerBooks.com

RichardBell@BusinessManagerBooks.com

www.ingramcontent.com/pod-product-compliance
Lightning Source LLC
Chambersburg PA
CBHW051319170526
45166CB00002B/612